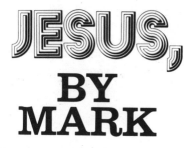

JESUS,
BY
MARK

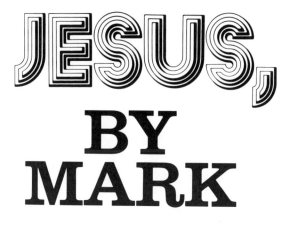

JESUS, BY MARK

Paul B. Smith

WELCH PUBLISHING COMPANY INC.
Burlington, Ontario, Canada

All scripture quotations in *Jesus, By Mark* are taken from the King James Version of The Holy Bible unless otherwise indicated.

ISBN: 1-55011-011-X

© 1987 by Paul B. Smith

Welch Publishing Company Inc.
960 The Gateway
Burlington, Ontario
L7L 5K7 Canada

Printed in Canada

To Sue Gerard

Who sang these sermons into the hearts of the people. When I first brought this series on Mark, each message was concluded by Sue with an appropriate song. Sometimes when I felt that my words had missed the mark, Sue Gerard's message hit it. Thanks, Sue!

Thanks also to my daughter, Jann, who worked many late hours transcribing these messages.

CONTENTS

Foreword   9

Introduction   11

Part One   Chapter 1 — He Preaches a Sermon   17
             Chapter 2 — He Heals a Cripple   25
             Chapter 3 — He Limits God's Forgiveness   33

Part Two   Chapter 4 — The Farmer and the Soil   43
             Chapter 5 — The Woman and the Tassel   49
             Chapter 6 — The Boy and the Lunch   57

Part Three   Chapter 7 — From Tradition to the Word   69
             Chapter 8 — From Blindness to Sight   75
             Chapter 9 — From Earth to Heaven   85

Part Four   Chapter 10 — A Goodness That Doesn't Save   97
             Chapter 11 — A Shortcut That Leads to Nowhere   101
             Chapter 12 — A Recklessness That Pleases God   107

Part Five   Chapter 13 — Ingredients in Life—Not Signs   121
             Chapter 14 — Impulsive Love—Not Calculated   133
             Chapter 15 — Political Career—Not Sound
                          Judgment   141

Part Six   Chapter 16 — Looking in the Wrong Places for
                          the Right Person   151

Foreword

As a young man, I spoke in Toronto, Canada, for a Saturday night Youth For Christ service held at The Peoples Church. After the meeting, Dr. Oswald J. Smith, the renowned pastor and church leader, asked me to stay over for Sunday evening to be the guest speaker at the church. Years passed and Dr. Smith's son, Dr. Paul Smith, conducted a missionary conference for my son, H. B. London, Jr., and his great church in Salem, Oregon. At that conference my son really caught the vision of the Great Commission. He called and encouraged me to have Paul Smith at California Graduate School of Theology, which we did many times, and each time we were blessed and our love for missions increased.

Since that time I have been honored to be in his pulpit every year for the past ten years.

There is no man that I have ever met who is more dedicated to God and concerned about getting the gospel to all the nations of the world than is Paul Smith. His book *Jesus, By Mark* is one of the most interesting, exciting and informative that you will ever have the privilege of reading. It should be in the hands of every minister and layman in the Western world. The first chapter will inspire you as he talks about Jesus when he preached his first sermon; and he talks about the many things Jesus did: overcame temptation, called his first disciple, cast out devils, healed the sick and raised the dead.

When this book is available, I am personally going to send twenty-five copies to fellow ministers of the gospel. In reading this book, you will be made to magnify the greatness of our Lord.

Dr. Paul Smith has been a leader and pastor of The Peoples Church for many years. I consider him one of the ten most outstanding preachers and church leaders throughout Canada and America.

Holland B. London, Sr.
Chancellor of the California Graduate School of Theology

Introduction

John Mark was a young man in a hurry. In the King James Version of the Bible he took only sixteen chapters to tell his story, whereas John took twenty-one, Luke twenty-four, and Matthew twenty-eight. Sources from the middle of the second century tell us that he was nicknamed "Stumpy-fingered." The Greek word would be *kolobodaktulos*. It is unlikely that it had anything to do with the length of his fingers—anymore than General George Patton's nickname during the Second World War, "Blood and Guts," had anything to do with his anatomy, or heavyweight boxer Joe Louis' nickname, "The Brown Bomber," had anything to do with explosives.

The fact is that Mark said only what was necessary in order to tell his story. He did not elaborate on the details or on the teaching. He was "stumpy-fingered" in his manner of writing. He was a young man in a hurry.

Certainly he was very literally in a great hurry when the people who had arrested Jesus attempted to arrest him as well. He ran off, leaving the linen cloth (which seemed to be the only thing that he was wearing at the time) in their hands (Mark 16:50-65). At least Mark was still around after all the "official" disciples had made good their escape.

John Mark's mother, Mary, was a wealthy woman who probably came from Cyprus. She lived in Jerusalem and her home seemed to be the gathering place for the disciples during the early years. Apparently Peter felt quite confident about finding them there after his miraculous escape from prison (Acts 12:12). It is possible that this was the home where the Last Supper was held and perhaps the place where 120 Christians met for prayer on the day of Pentecost.

Although he was about ten years younger than most of the disciples, Mark was closely associated with both Paul and Peter. He accompanied the apostle Paul on his first missionary journey as a kind of assistant. Halfway through this trip Mark decided to go back to Jerusalem instead of continuing with them to Antioch, Iconium and other cities in Asia.

On the second missionary journey Paul refused to take Mark with them because, said Paul, "He went not with them to the work." So there was a division between Paul and Barnabas: "The contention was so sharp between them, that they departed asunder one from the other" (Acts 15:39). So Barnabas broke with Paul and took Mark with him back to Cyprus while the apostle Paul set out for Syria and Cilicia with Silas.

This incident may explain Paul's "thorn in the flesh" better than any other. Paul was probably a very difficult man to work with. His besetting sins may have been arrogance and self-righteousness, and perhaps he knew that if he didn't guard himself every moment he would fall into them very easily. It is interesting to notice how often he comes very close to bragging both about his background and education and about the model life he had lived. Remember, he had been a Pharisee—one of the best:

> For Christ sent me not to baptize, but to preach the gospel: not with wisdom of words, lest the cross of Christ should be made of none effect (1 Cor. 1:17).

> And I, brethren, when I came to you, came not with excellency of speech or of wisdom, declaring unto you the testimony of God. For I determined not to know anything among you, save Jesus Christ, and him crucified. And I was with you in weakness, and in fear, and in much trembling. And my speech and my preaching was not with enticing words of man's wisdom, but in demonstration of the Spirit and of power (1 Cor. 2:1-4).

> And I, brethren, could not speak unto you as unto spiritual, but as unto carnal, even as unto babes in Christ. I have fed you with milk, and not with meat: for hitherto ye were not able to bear it, neither yet now are ye able (1 Cor. 3:1-2).

> Am I not an apostle? am I not free? have I not seen Jesus Christ our Lord? are not ye my work in the Lord? If I be not an apostle unto others, yet doubtless I am to you: for the seal of mine apostleship are ye in the Lord (1 Cor. 9:1-2).

> Even as I please all men in all things, not seeking mine own profit, but the profit of many, that they may be saved (1 Cor. 10:33).

> Though I speak with the tongues of men and of angels . . . and though I have the gift of prophecy, and understand all mysteries, and all knowledge; and though I have all faith, so that I could remove mountains . . . and though I bestow all my goods to feed the poor, and though I give my body to be burned, and have not charity, it profiteth me nothing (1 Cor. 13:1-3).

> But in all things approving ourselves as the ministers of God, in much patience, in afflictions, in necessities, in distresses, in stripes, in imprisonments, in tumults, in labours, in watchings, in fastings, by pureness,

by knowledge, by longsuffering, by kindness, by the Holy Ghost, by love unfeigned, by the word of truth, by the power of God, by the armour of righteousness on the right hand and on the left, by honour and dishonour, by evil report and good report: as deceivers, and yet true; as unknown, and yet well known; as dying, and, behold, we live; as chastened, and not killed; as sorrowful, yet always rejoicing; as poor, yet making many rich; as having nothing, and yet possessing all things (2 Cor. 6:4-10).

Receive us; we have wronged no man, we have corrupted no man, we have defrauded no man (2 Cor. 7:2).

Are they Hebrews? So am I. Are they Israelites? So am I. Are they the seed of Abraham? So am I. Are they ministers of Christ? . . . I am more; in labours more abundant, in stripes above measure, in prisons more frequent, in deaths oft. Of the Jews five times received I forty stripes save one. Thrice was I beaten with rods, once I was stoned, thrice I suffered shipwreck, a night and a day I have been in the deep; in journeyings often, in perils of water, in perils of robbers, in perils by mine own countrymen, in perils by the heathen, in perils in the city, in perils in the wilderness, in perils in the sea, in perils among false brethren; in weariness and painfulness, in watchings often, in hunger and thirst, in fastings often, in cold and nakedness. Besides those things that are without, that which cometh upon me daily, the care of all the churches. Who is weak, and I am not weak? Who is offended, and I burn not? If I must needs glory, I will glory of the things which concern mine infirmities (2 Cor. 11:22-30).

Therefore I take pleasure in infirmities, in reproaches, in necessities, in persecutions, in distresses for Christ's sake; for when I am weak, then am I strong. I am become a fool in glorying; ye have compelled me: for I ought to have been commanded of you: for in nothing am I behind the very chiefest apostles, though I be nothing (2 Cor. 12:10-11).

Though I might also have confidence in the flesh. If any other man thinketh that he hath whereof he might trust in the flesh, I more, . . . (Phil. 3:4).

For yourselves know how ye ought to follow us: for we behaved not ourselves disorderly among you; neither did we eat any man's bread for nought; but wrought with labour and travail night and day, that we might not be chargeable to any of you; not because we have not power, but to make ourselves an ensample unto you to follow us (2 Thess. 3:7-9).

But thou hast fully known my doctrine, manner of life, purpose, faith, longsuffering, charity, patience, persecutions, afflictions, which came unto me at Antioch, at Iconium, at Lystra; what persecutions I endure: but out of them all the Lord delivered me. Yea, and all that will live godly in Christ Jesus shall suffer persecution (2 Tim. 3:10-12).

Can you imagine how difficult it would be to work with a man like the apostle Paul? He had an unbelievable background of human accomplishment and an equally horrendous trail of sacrifices for Jesus Christ. He was obviously very much aware of both, but he had managed to put them to one side and consider himself little more than a piece of dirt; and I don't think this was at all phony or unreal. He knew he was something, a very big something, but he looked upon himself as nothing—a nothing so small that a high-powered microscope would have had difficulty finding it.

This was fine for the apostle Paul, but I imagine that he expected everybody on his team to live up to his own standards. By the time they had gone only halfway on their first missionary journey, the youthful John Mark had had it up to the eyebrows with the apostle Paul. I think he must have been saying words to the effect, "I don't want him. You can have him. He's too much for me."

Later in both of their lives Paul and Mark got together again. By this time Mark had probably matured a great deal and perhaps the apostle Paul had become a little bit more understanding. At any rate, when Paul writes to Timothy from Rome, he asks him to bring Mark along when he comes to Rome, "for he is profitable to me for the ministry" (2 Timothy 4:11).

John Mark's association with the apostle Peter had probably been much more intimate—although we do not know as much about it as we do about his relationship with Paul. However, it would appear that Mark may have been a convert of Peter's who joined him in Rome, heard him preach many times and, after Peter's death, undertook to put Peter's messages in writing. This is the Gospel of Mark, probably written in Rome with Gentile people as its target. In all probability it represents an accurate reproduction of the teaching of the apostle Peter.

Part One

He Preaches a Sermon — Chapter 1
He Heals a Cripple — Chapter 2
He Limits God's Forgiveness — Chapter 3

/

And immediately the spirit driveth him into the wilderness. And he was there in the wilderness forty days, tempted of Satan; and was with the wild beasts; and the angels ministered unto him. Now after that John was put in prison, Jesus came into Galilee, preaching the gospel of the kingdom of God, and saying, "The time is fulfilled, and the kingdom of God is at hand: repent ye, and believe the gospel."

Mark 1:12-15

Chapter 1

He Preaches a Sermon

In my book *Jesus, by John* I attempted to answer the question, Who was he? and focussed on those verses in each chapter that showed how John saw Jesus in that particular chapter: he was the Creator, he was the Creature, he was the Counsellor, and so on throughout the twenty-one chapters. In contrast to the apostle John, Mark was an extremely active man, and he wrote down the words of a very active person, Peter. For this reason I am going to look at each of Mark's chapters and ask the question, What did he do?

He Preached His First Sermon

In the forty-five verses of this first chapter Mark races through a great many things that Jesus did; he offers himself for baptism, he over-

17

comes temptation, he calls his first disciples, he teaches in the synagogue, he casts out a devil, he heals many people, including Peter's mother-in-law, he establishes his pattern of early morning prayer, he demonstrates the missionary principle by refusing to stay in one town and he heals a leper.

In addition to all of these other things he preaches his first sermon: "Now after that John was put in prison, Jesus came into Galilee, preaching the gospel of the kingdom of God, and saying, 'The time was fulfilled, and the kingdom of God is at hand: repent ye, and believe the gospel' " (Mark 1:14-15).

The contents of the sermon are not actually given but even a casual survey of the New Testament would indicate that when Mark introduces Jesus Christ to the world, he is presenting the one who stands between man and all of his basic fears.

The Fear of Death

It is absolutely amazing what man will go through, put up with or do to keep from dying. One of the most amazing stories in marine history is the incredible voyage of Captain William Bligh and eighteen members of his crew after the mutiny on his ship, the *Bounty*, in 1789. Bligh was able to navigate with this motley crew a distance of nearly four thousand miles from Tonga to Timor in an open boat. The men went through such terrible hardships on this trip that it is difficult to understand why they did not jump overboard and drown peacefully in the sea rather than endure what they did before arriving at their destination. The only answer is that we human beings have an insatiable desire to live; anything is better than death. That is why the gospel message is so important. "And this is the record, that God has given to us eternal life, and this life is in his Son" (1 John 5:11).

Jesus Christ removes our fear of death.

Fear of Judgment

We don't really need a Bible to tell us that our wickedness will catch up with us. The universality of religion is evidence of the fact that we believe that no one gets away with anything and that at some point we will suffer for the evil we have done. When the tribes of Gad and Reuben came to Moses to request that they be permitted to remain on the eastern

18

side of the river Jordan, his answer was that they could do so—but only if their men of war crossed the river and helped the rest of the tribes fight the battles in the Promised Land. It was in this connection that Moses said that if they did not do so they would be committing a sin against God, and he reminded them that they would not be able to hide it. "But if ye will not do so, behold, ye have sinned against the Lord: and be sure your sin will find you out" (Num. 32:23).

"Your sin will find you out." I don't think this was news to these people. Moses was simply reminding them of something they already knew. And this is true of all people everywhere. It seems that men and women have an instinct which states this as a universal principle, so that people everywhere are afraid of judgment. In different societies the form this will take and who will bring it about changes, depending on their religious persuasion, but it remains a principle common to all mankind.

The apostle Paul made it clear to the church at Rome: "For what the law could not do, in that it was weak through the flesh, God sending his own Son in the likeness of sinful flesh, and for sin, condemned sin in the flesh" (Rom. 8:3).

John was able to say, "He that believeth on him (Jesus) is not condemned: but he that believeth not is condemned already, because he hath not believed in the name of the only begotten Son of God" (John 3:18).

Jesus Christ has made it possible for our sin to be removed: "As far as the east is from the west, so far hath he removed our transgressions from us" (Ps. 103:12). David wrote this, but he did not know how or when it would be accomplished. In Jesus Christ we have no fear of judgment because when we trust him as our Savior, our sin is removed.

Jesus Christ makes it possible for our sin to be buried: "Thou wilt cast all their sins into the depths of the sea" (Mic. 7:19). Micah proclaimed this but, once again, he did not know how it would be accomplished.

Finally, Jesus Christ makes it possible for our sins to be put right out of sight; "Thou hast cast all my sins behind thy back" (Isa. 38:17). Isaiah makes an even stronger declaration when he says, "Though your sins be as scarlet, they shall be as white as snow; though they be red like crimson, they shall be as wool" (Isa. 1:18).

Not only are our sins out of sight, but they have also been washed away. From our standpoint, something that had been put behind our backs might be brought out again at some time in the future, but the Bible makes it very clear that our sins are gone. It is as if they had never existed. God doesn't even remember that we have sinned. "For I will be merciful to their unrighteousness, and their sins and their iniquities will I

19

remember no more" (Heb. 8:12).

This is very difficult for us to understand. We do not have the ability to deliberately forget anything. When a person has offended us we may forgive that person, but the memory of what they have done will always be in our minds. Just as God was able to create the world out of nothing, so he is able to reverse that process and, to coin a phrase, "uncreate" anything. This is what he does with our sins when we confess them and trust Jesus Christ as our Savior—he "uncreates" our sins. That is, they no longer exist.

When I was a small boy we used to sing a chorus:

> Gone, gone, gone, gone, yes my sins are gone,
> Buried in the deepest sea,
> Yes that's good enough for me;
> I shall live eternally;
> Praise God my sins are gone!

When I sang this in Sunday school as a child, I didn't really understand how totally impossible this is to our minds. This chorus is talking about the "uncreating" power of God. We simply do not understand it, but in faith we accept it.

Jesus Christ removes the fear of judgment by totally obliterating our sins.

The Fear of Being Inadequate

"He that spared not his own Son, but delivered him up for us all, how shall he not with him also freely give us all things?" (Rom. 8:32).

Among other things this verse assures us that under any circumstances God will give us whatever we need. We are his children, and therefore he has obligated himself to look after us. He may not give us as much as we think we should have or as much as other people may have, but he understands the basic needs of his own children. We never have to concern ourselves about whether or not we have sufficient to satisfy our needs or whether we have the necessary ability to do whatever God has called us to do. When we trust Jesus Christ as our Savior, he removes the fear of inadequacy.

The Fear of Being an Outcast

"Now then we are ambassadors for Christ, as though God did beseech you by us: we pray you in Christ's stead, be ye reconciled to God" (2 Cor. 5:20).

"Be ye reconciled to God" means settle your quarrel with God, so that once again there can be a spirit of friendship between you and God. This is what we mean when we urge people to "get right with God!"

It hurts our spirits when we have a misunderstanding with a friend, and when we do, we should make every effort to settle the matter—that is, to be reconciled with our friend. It is even more depressing to have a quarrel with God and to go through life as an outcast. This is one of our great fears—the fear of being an outcast from God and from the family of God. When we trust Jesus Christ as our Savior, there is a sense in which we are approaching God with a white flag. We are tired of maintaining the quarrel and we are anxious to get the matter settled.

What the average person does not realize is that God is even more anxious than we are for us to become reconciled to him. As a matter of fact, it is God who makes the first move. Paul says that he is speaking in the name of God, who "beseeches us" to be reconciled in the name of Jesus Christ.

Because of what Jesus Christ has done, it is no longer necessary to be an enemy of God. We no longer have to be outcasts. We can be reconciled, and the fear of being an outcast can be removed.

The Fear of Being Bad

Immediately following this verse about reconciliation, the apostle Paul says a word about why it is necessary to be reconciled with God: "For he hath made him to be sin for us, who knew no sin; that we might be made the righteousness of God in him" (2 Cor. 5:21).

It is sin that stands between us and God. In other words, in the eyes of God we are bad people. Whenever I read our Lord's comment about Nathanael I think how much I would like to be that kind of a man: "Jesus saw Nathanael coming to him, and saith of him, Behold an Israelite indeed, in whom is no guile!" (John 1:47). But that is impossible, of course, because I am bad. I know myself better than anybody else in the world knows me. I am aware of how very far I am from measuring up to God's standard of righteousness. I simply cannot be good because I was born bad.

21

Wonder of wonders, the very opposite is true. Even though I have been born bad, I do not have to stay bad. Jesus Christ can make me good. He completely removes the fear of being bad.

The Fear of Belonging to the Wrong Family

"But when the fulness of the time was come, God sent forth his Son, made of a woman, made under the law, to redeem them that were under the law, that we might receive the adoption of sons" (Gal. 4:4-5).

Our word adoption comes from the Latin *adoptare*, which means "to desire" or "to choose." An adopted child always has this slight edge over the natural children in a family: the adopted child was chosen. Sometimes the natural child was not even wanted, let alone chosen. In the case of God's family, it is God who deliberately has chosen us to be members of his family because that is what he wanted.

The Bible says, "He hath chosen us in him before the foundation of the world, that we should be holy and without blame before him in love" (Eph. 1:4). It is very difficult for us to understand all that may be involved in a statement like this, but at least it means that we can be members of the family of God—and that, by way of adoption. He has chosen us.

The family to which we belong can make a great difference in our lives. It is our family that determines where we are born, how much of this world's goods we have with which to start life, and who the people will be that form our society. Many of these things can be changed afterwards, but the family into which we are born influences our future probably more than any other one factor. It is a decided asset to be born into the right family. It can be a terrible handicap to be born into the wrong family. Man has a fear of belonging to the wrong family—a fear that is removed by Jesus Christ.

The Fear of a Futile Life

"For we are his workmanship, created in Christ Jesus unto good works, which God hath before ordained that we should walk in them" (Eph. 2:10).

There are some people who have difficulty climbing out of bed in the morning because they think that there is nothing worth getting up for. Their lives are filled with useless activities, and each day brings new activities that are equally useless.

The Bible tells us that it is not necessary to live this kind of life. We can rise every morning to face a day that will be filled with "good works"—that is, filled with those kinds of things that will be profitable to us, profitable to others, and looked upon as profitable by God. Jesus Christ removes the fear of living a futile life.

The Fear of Being Left Penniless

"That being justified by his grace, we should be made heirs according to the hope of eternal life" (Titus 3:7).

It is the fear of being left penniless that the Amway Corporation uses to enlist its salespeople. They usually launch their appeal by saying, "This is a career that can assure you of financial security." This statement will then be followed by the testimonies of people who have arrived at this state of "financial security" by selling Amway products.

There are very few people in the world who do not respond to this kind of a proposition. We do not want to be left penniless, and the only way to be sure that this does not happen to us is to develop some sort of financial security. Of course, one of the best ways to do this is to belong to a wealthy family—to become an heir of great wealth.

Let me hasten to say that when the Bible talks of our rights as heirs of God, it is not necessarily speaking of material wealth. It is true that there are some Christians who have become wealthy. However, any real knowledge of the world would lead us to the conclusion that, in most cases, Christians are not wealthy people. As a matter of fact, it is generally because they *are* Christians that they *are not* wealthy. There is no guarantee of financial security in this world for the Christian. (The facts of life prove that this is not so, and anyone who believes it does not know very much about the world.)

However, when we become Christians we fall heir to all the wealth of God after this life is over. The apostle Peter was never an affluent man and he died the death of a martyr. Nevertheless, he was able to write to the church of his day and say this: "Blessed be the God and Father of our Lord Jesus Christ, which according to his abundant mercy hath begotten us again unto a lively hope by the resurrection of Jesus Christ from the dead, to an inheritance incorruptible, and undefiled, and that fadeth not away, reserved in heaven for you" (1 Peter 1:3-4).

Christianity brings blessing and prosperity, but in most cases that is not to be reckoned in financial terms or in material possessions. In the

23

United States and Canada we are the exception to the international rule. By far the majority of Christians throughout the world are poor, and they will always be poor. The inheritance to which we look forward is in heaven. Because of Jesus Christ, the fear of being left penniless is removed. We are the children of the King and we will inherit an unimaginable fortune—not now, but afterwards.

Conclusion

There are eight fears that the gospel of Christ removes: 1) the fear of death, 2) the fear of judgment, 3) the fear of being inadequate, 4) the fear of being an outcast, 5) the fear of being bad, 6) the fear of belonging to the wrong family, 7) the fear of living a futile life, and 8) the fear of being left penniless.

In the first chapter of Mark we have the simple statement that "Jesus came into Galilee, preaching the gospel of the kingdom of God." This is the gospel, and in this book Mark is going to introduce us to the Person who came into this world to make the gospel possible.

And again he entered into Capernaum after some days; and it was noised that he was in the house. And straightaway many were gathered together, insomuch that there was no room to receive them, no, not so much as about the door: and he preached the word unto them. And they come unto him, bringing one sick of the palsy, which was borne of four. And when they could not come nigh unto him for the press, they uncovered the roof where he was: and when they had broken it up, they let down the bed wherein the sick of the palsy lay. When Jesus saw their faith, he said unto the sick of the palsy, "Son, thy sins be forgiven thee."

Mark 2:1-5

Chapter 2

He Heals a Cripple

It would be impossible to argue against mass evangelism from the ministry of our Lord because he did a great deal of it—particularly in the earlier part of his work. Constantly he was besieged by multitudes so that on one occasion he had to get into a small boat in order to have room enough to teach the crowds that had come to hear him. On the other hand, Jesus did a great deal of person-to-person evangelism where it was a case of one on one. Jesus' ministry seemed to be divided between an effective use of both methods.

The story that Mark relates in the first part of his second chapter would not have been told if it had not been for the huge crowd that had blocked all of the entrances to the house where Jesus was teaching. "And straightway many were gathered together, insomuch that there was no room to receive them, no, not so much as about the door: and he preached the word unto them" (Mark 2:2).

The composition of our Lord's crowds was about the same as you

25

would expect to find in any modern religious service. There were critics. Mark mentions the scribes. In Luke's account of the same incident he refers to Pharisees and doctors of the law. They were professional religious critics—and there are some of these in every religious crowd of any size. They do not come to be blessed; they come to find fault. Luke names these people and then says, "And the power of the Lord was present to heal them" (Luke 5:17). Jesus was just as anxious to help them as he was to help anybody else, but that is not what they wanted. Therefore they left the presence of our Lord pretty much unchanged.

In the Savior's crowds there were also the faithful. A few years after this incident the apostle Paul was going to refer to these people as "pillars" (Gal. 2:9). The faithful in Jesus' audiences would include his disciples and a few women who were sometimes stronger in their support of him than even the disciples. Remember that the disciples completely forsook him after the crucifixion, but the women were still close by—actually at the foot of the cross, and then watching Joseph of Arimathaea and Nicodemus bury him. These faithful women were the first at the tomb on the day of resurrection. Every spiritual ministry has its small group of devout backers. It is these "pillars" that give God's servants the strength they need to withstand the critics, and every good ministry has them.

Finally, there were always the common people. This was by far the largest group. These were the people who had come to listen to what Jesus had to say out of curiosity. These were the people of Galilee, which was looked upon contemptuously by the Jews who lived in the southern part of Palestine. (Palestine itself was considered backward and unimportant by the Romans. The last place on earth in which a Roman soldier would want to be stationed was the land of the Jews.) Often these common people would come and listen to the teaching of Jesus in hope that he might perform a miracle, relieving the monotony of their existence.

The ordinary people who formed our Lord's crowds were also bewildered. On one occasion Jesus said, "They were as sheep not having a shepherd." They seemed to have no purpose in their lives—no objective, no reason for living. They came to listen to Jesus because here was a teacher who might give them a reason to go on living.

Of course the crowds that followed Jesus were always hungry—spiritually hungry. They were looking for something that would satisfy the needs of their hearts. The story in Mark, chapter two centers around four men who wanted to get a sick friend to Jesus. The King James Version describes this man's illness as "the palsy." Palsy is a contracted form of the word paralysis. We are told very little about the kind of paralysis he had except that it must have been severe enough so that he was unable to walk by himself and had to be carried on a bed. Still, his four friends were determined to get this paralytic to Jesus.

If we want to learn how to bring a difficult case within the sound of the gospel and therefore exposed to the message of Jesus Christ, there is no better illustration to be found anywhere in the Bible. The four friends could have come up with many reasons as to why they could not do it. One, he can't walk. Most of us would have stopped there. Two, there is an enormous crowd: he will be jostled and he will probably be hurt more than he will be helped. Three, even if we do succeed in getting him through the crowd, it may not do him any good.

Fortunately for this crippled man, his friends were *positive thinkers*. They did not even ask the question: Is there a way? Assuming there was a way, they proceeded to look for it, and they found it.

People who leave an imprint on the sands of time for God are those who go ahead regardless of the impossibilities. I think Zacchaeus was such a man. One day when Jesus was passing through Jericho, Zacchaeus decided that he must see him. However, he had two serious problems. For one thing, he was short of stature and of course, as usual, the crowd was enormous. He was simply not able to see over top of them. However, perhaps more serious than this was the fact that he was a tax collector for the Roman government. The Jews hated any Jew who took money from the Romans for any kind of service—particularly tax collectors, or publicans, as Luke calls them. This meant that nobody would think of moving over so that Zacchaeus could get up to the front of the line. He was a despised man.

However, Zacchaeus was not about to be put off. Although his legs were short, he was still able to run. He raced ahead of where the major crowd was congesting the streets, then climbed up into a sycamore tree so that when Jesus came by he would be able to look down on him.

The result was that he was the only person in that crowd that Jesus honored by having lunch with them. Here was a man whose name has gone down in history because he had the determination to overcome his shortcomings.

I think Samson was a similar man. I have always been intrigued by the story of how Samson killed a thousand Philistines using only the jawbone of a donkey. Samson was no stranger to the power of the Spirit of God. At Timnath he had killed a lion with his bare hands and at Ashkelon he had killed thirty men. However, this was something different. The odds were a thousand to one against him. I don't believe that

27

Samson thought for one single moment that he would be able to kill that many warriors. But he knew that he was God's man and they were God's enemies and that it was his responsibility to swing a blow for God.

Unfortunately, he had no weapons with him. He looked around. There, close to his feet, a donkey had died and the birds had already eaten away the flesh. Samson reached down and took hold of the donkey's jawbone and lifted it. I am sure that the thought must have gone through his mind, "This is a strange sort of weapon. I wonder what my sword instructor would say about this?" Then he looked up and he noticed that one of the Philistines was making better time in his direction than the others. He knew he had nine hundred and ninety-nine men behind him. Samson swung the jawbone, killed the leading Philistine, then shoved him to one side. When he brought his arm back up again there was another Philistine, standing right in front of him. Again he swung the jawbone, killed the Philistine and moved him over on top of the first. This process went on for quite some time. You see, all that Samson actually did was kill one Philistine at a time, and God lined up the others until, at length, he had killed the last one of a thousand.

You see the problem with most of us is that we are defeated by the nine hundred and ninety-nine obstacles that haven't reached us yet and we fail to deal with the one that is directly in front of us. Certainly the Spirit of God had come upon Samson, but he used the power that God gave him to the greatest possible advantage.

There is often something quite unorthodox about the people who have accomplished great things in the service of God. When John Wesley was no longer permitted to preach in the Church of England, he went outside and used his grandmother's tombstone in Epworth to preach to thousands of people in the open air.

George Whitefield came to America and did what today we would think quite impossible—he spoke to ten thousand people on the Boston Commons without benefit of a microphone or a loudspeaker.

Imagine the courage of Martin Luther when he took his stand against the entire Roman Catholic church and nailed his thesis to the door of All Saints' Church in Wittenberg Cathedral.

It was certainly unorthodox and a bit shocking when Billy Sunday took off his suit coat and stood in his shirtsleeves on top of the pulpit instead of behind it to preach to thousands of people, but this is the kind of thing God seems to honor.

William Carey, sometimes called the father of modern missions, put it well, "Attempt great things for God; expect great things from God."

Two thousand years ago four men attempted something great. They were determined that in some way they would get their sick friend to Jesus. It is worth noting that the four of them by combining their efforts were able to do something that no one of them could have done by himself. It took four, one at each corner of the bed, to lift the man and carry him. This principle is still true in the work of getting people to Christ. There are very few converts who were brought to the Savior by any one person. Generally there is a chain of events, a series of circumstances, a number of people—all of whom bring their influence to bear before any one sinner who is converted.

Sometimes a man comes under the influence of an Apollos—a Billy Sunday with his gift of oratory. This moves him towards Christ, but not all the way. Later on he is confronted by an apostle Paul—a G. Campbell Morgan with his great teaching ability. The word of God begins to take on a meaning that he has never before been able to grasp and he is moved closer to Christ; but he does not respond yet.

Then he may come under the influence of a Cephas—a Jonathan Edwards that thunders out the judgment of God against unrepentant sinners. He is moved closer still, but the time has not yet come when he repents and comes to Christ. Finally, he hears someone like the apostle John—a Gypsy Smith with his appeal of love and mercy. Wonder of wonders, he responds and is saved.

Who won him to Christ? Was it Apollos? No! Was it Paul? No! Was it Cephas? No! Was it John? No! It was all four. Each one picked up one corner of the man's couch and lifted, and with their combined efforts they got him to Jesus.

If you have an unsaved friend, you may not be able to win him to Christ by yourself. You may have to find three other friends who will covenant together with you to pray for your friend and use every means that they can possibly bring to bear upon him to get him to Christ. What you have not been able to do by yourself, you and your three friends may accomplish under the anointing of the Spirit of God.

The final barrier these four men had to face was the huge crowd. However, now that they had carried their friend this far, they were not going to be stopped by the people. I imagine they had a short consultation. Somebody suggested that they could let him down through the roof, into the middle of the crowd and right before the Savior. This is the point at which anyone who had been completely orthodox would have said, "Excuse me, this is where I get off"; but these were not orthodox men. They climbed up on the roof carrying their friend—not an easy task. Then they must have found four pieces of rope which they tied to the corners of the bed. Then they let him down in front of Jesus right in the middle of our Lord's discourse. Can you imagine how shocked the doctors of the law and the Pharisees and the scribes must have been? They must have thought it was absolutely outrageous. But it didn't seem to phase Jesus at all. He calmly turned to the crippled man and said, "Son, thy sins be forgiven thee" (Mark 2:5).

Whereupon the critics, who had been looking for an opportunity to find fault with Jesus' teaching, jumped in with both feet, so to speak, and cried out in protest: "Who does this man think he is? Doesn't he know that only God can forgive sins? This is blasphemy, because he is attempting to do what only God is able to do."

Our Lord was not the least bit upset. He went on calmly speaking, first to the critics and then to the man himself: "But that ye may know that the Son of man hath power on earth to forgive sins, (he saith to the sick of the palsy,) I say unto thee, Arise, and take up thy bed, and go thy way into thine house. And immediately he arose, took up the bed, and went forth before them all; insomuch that they were all amazed, and glorified God, saying, We never saw it on this fashion" (Mark 2:10-12).

Jesus obviously felt that the man's spiritual need was much more important than his physical need because he dealt with it first. Very often we get this order reversed. Spiritual healing is only incidental to physical healing. When we call upon the Lord he saves us—every time. There are no exceptions. When we ask God for the healing of our bodies, sometimes he does it, but most of the time he does not. If he healed every Christian who asked him to do so, there would not be any sick Christians. Furthermore, Christians would never die, because death always involves some kind of sickness, a breakdown of some vital area of our bodily functions.

I am sure that the saints in the first-century church cried out to God to preserve them from martyrdom, but generally God did not choose to answer that prayer. As a matter of fact, in the Book of Revelation the way in which God's people will overcome the Antichrist will not be by *deliverance* from death; their victory will be gained *through* their deaths.

We cannot command God. The spiritual health of God's people is what is vitally important. Their physical health is a secondary matter. In the case of the paralytic, Jesus finally healed him physically as well as spiritually so that he was able to take up his bed and walk home.

We would have failed utterly in our comments about this passage if we did not point out the fact that the best way to bring glory to God is to find means by which to get people under the sound of the gospel of Christ so that they have a chance to be saved.

No one could adequately describe the glory given to God because of this man's experience. Mark tells us that they all glorified God. Of course that would include the casual onlookers and listeners—the people. They glorified God by telling everybody they saw within the next few days what a wonderful thing had happened. This increased the size of the crowds that followed Jesus and gave him many more people to talk to. This brought glory to God.

I am sure that this would also include the disciples. They had given up everything to follow Jesus, and sometimes I imagine that some of them may have got up that morning a little bit discouraged, perhaps wondering if it had been worth it all. The salvation and healing of this paralytic must have reassured them. That glorified God.

There is no doubt in my mind that the four men who had brought their sick friend to Jesus must have had great difficulty in containing their emotions. I think that perhaps one of them must have said, "Praise the Lord. Let's go and bring another friend to Jesus"—and the glory went up to God.

Luke tells us in his Gospel that the man himself went away glorifying God. I imagine that he rolled up his bed, put it up on his shoulders and began to push his way through the huge crowd, saying, "Get out of my way. I came in lying on this bed and I am going out carrying the bed on my shoulder. Glory to God!"

Did the man have a family? If he did, they probably glorified God more than anybody else. I sometimes imagine a young mother with three small children in a little house on the outskirts of town. She had done most of the work that she had to do on the morning of this miraculous day, and she was sitting on a chair in the front room. As she looked back over her life, a deep sigh escaped her lips as she thought about the trials that she had been through. In a room at the back of the ramshackle house lay her young husband—a cripple, totally useless. The children were off in some other part of the house playing. She had very little to look forward to.

As she sat there, there was a knock at the front door. She walked wearily to the door. There stood four of her husband's friends. They told her that Jesus was in town and that they would like to take her husband to see him. Maybe Jesus could heal him. I think the tired young woman sighed once again and said, "It will probably not do much good, but go ahead if you wish."

They immediately went in to see their sick friend, told him what they wanted to do and, when he agreed, they picked up his bed and carried him out of the house.

Late in the afternoon of that same day there was another knock on the front door. When she trudged over and opened it, she saw a stranger standing there. No, he was not a stranger; it was her husband. But she didn't recognize him because he hadn't looked that well for a long time—ever since that dreadful paralysis had struck him. But now she saw that it was he. There he stood with his bed on his shoulder. She was absolutely speechless.

Her husband threw the bed to one side, strode into the room, picked his wife up in his arms and said, "Where are the children? Go and tell them they've got a new daddy. I went to see Jesus today and he forgave me for all of my sins and restored my body to its normal condition." The children were called and they too were speechless, clinging to their father's pant leg as he continued to hold their mother in his arms: "Let's kneel down and pray."

It had been a long, long time since they had done this, and he had almost forgotten how to pray. But I think that perhaps if he had been living in our times, he might have offered the simple prayer of the little child:

> Gentle Jesus meek and mild,
> Look upon a little child;
> Pity my simplicity;
> Suffer me to come to thee.

And the glory went up to God!

And the scribes which came down from Jerusalem said, "He hath Beelzebub, and by the prince of the devils casteth he out devils." And he called them unto him, and said unto them in parables, "How can Satan cast out Satan? And if a kingdom be divided against itself, that kingdom cannot stand. And if a house be divided against itself, that house cannot stand. And if Satan rise up against himself, and be divided, he cannot stand, but hath an end. No man can enter into a strong man's house, and spoil his goods, except he will first bind the strong man; and then he will spoil his house. Verily I say unto you, All sins shall be forgiven unto the sons of men, and blasphemies wherewith soever they shall blaspheme: But he that shall blaspheme against the Holy Ghost hath never forgiveness, but is in danger of eternal damnation:" Because they said, He hath an unclean spirit.

Mark 3:22-30

Chapter 3

He Limits God's Forgiveness

The most frightening passage in the Bible is the one in which our Lord tells us that there is a sin which even God cannot forgive. It is recorded by Matthew, Mark and Luke, but the incident occurred only one time: "Verily I say unto you, All sins shall be forgiven unto the sons of men, and blasphemies wherewith soever they shall blaspheme: But he that shall blaspheme against the Holy Ghost hath never forgiveness, but is in danger of eternal damnation" (Mark 3:28-29).

William Barclay calls this passage "a terrible saying." Dr. R. Allen Cole in the *Tyndale New Testament Commentary* refers to it as "one of the most solemn pronouncements and warnings in the whole of the New Testament."

One of the basic rules of Bible study is that we should never interpret an obscure passage at its face value if it contradicts other clear passages. What is this sin of "blasphemy against the Holy Ghost"? This is indeed a difficult saying, and perhaps the best way to get at its meaning is to look at the subject of forgiveness in the rest of the New Testament.

"For God so loved the world, that he gave his only begotten Son, that whosoever believeth in him should not perish, but have everlasting life" (John 3:16).

This golden text of the Bible declares that everlasting life is a possibility for an unqualified "whosoever." It does not say "whosoever has not committed the unpardonable sin"—only, "whosoever."

"Him that cometh to me I will in no wise cast out" (John 6:37). This passage uses an unqualified "him"—meaning any person in the world. It does not specify that only the one who has not committed the unpardonable sin may come. It only says "him"—without restrictions.

"Come unto me, all ye that labour and are heavy laden, and I will give you rest" (Matt. 11:28). In this passage our Lord is using an unqualified "all." He does not restrict it by saying "all who have not committed the unpardonable sin come unto me," but simply "all"—that is, anybody in the world.

"Whosoever will, let him take the water of life freely" (Rev. 22:17). Here is another of the Bible's many unqualified invitations. It does not say "whosoever will, let him take the water of life freely—as long as he has not committed the unpardonable sin." It is an invitation that is wide open to anybody in the world.

The New Testament is filled with such invitations. This means that anybody who has enough interest in being forgiven and will "believe," "come," or "take" can be forgiven—indeed, will be forgiven.

Putting this in reverse, we might say anyone who refuses to believe, to come, to take—cannot be forgiven. He cannot be forgiven because he has committed the unpardonable sin, that is, the sin of going through this life and being ushered into the next life without having taken advantage of God's offer of mercy and grasping it for himself.

In other words, the only unpardonable sin is the sin of rejecting Jesus Christ. There is no other. Not murder, not adultery, not homosexuality, not criticism, not pride, not jealousy—no, not any of these or any others we may have known or committed.

Having said that much, we must point out the fact that this offer of mercy is not open forever. The Bible makes it very clear that there is a time when God closes the door. There is a time when we have our last chance. There is a time when the justice of God takes over from the grace of God.

That is why it is so important to be sure that the decision has been made in our lives, and made in the right way.

"Now there is at Jerusalem by the sheep market a pool, which is called in the Hebrew tongue Bethesda, having five porches. In these lay a great multitude of impotent folk, of blind, halt, withered, waiting for the moving of the water. For an angel went down at a certain season into the pool, and troubled the water: whosoever then first after the troubling of the water stepped in was made whole of whatsoever disease he had" (John 5:2-4).

The story of the man at the pool at Bethesda is told only by John, but it is fascinating. If a sick person got into the pool when the angel troubled the waters, he would be cured of whatever malady he had. You may remember that the man with whom Jesus dealt in this story had been stricken with some disease for thirty-eight years. Apparently he had been lying close to the pool for some time but had never been able to get in when the waters were troubled.

Now let me take this story out of its context and apply it to the unpardonable sin. There are times in all of our lives when God troubles the waters. If we respond to the movement of the Holy Spirit at those times we will be saved. If we do not respond there is no guarantee that the waters will ever be troubled again.

There are many ways in which the Holy Spirit may trouble the waters of our lives. Sometimes he does it with sickness. Many times I've heard people testify to the effect that they had never thought very much about their relationship with God until they became seriously ill. Then, on a hospital bed for the first time in their lives, they realized their need and made whatever decision was necessary in order to be saved. What they are saying is that God troubled the waters in my life through sickness and I responded.

Testimonies we do not hear are from those who went through a very similar experience and when God troubled the waters, did not respond. Rather, their hearts became hardened and they refused to accept Jesus Christ as their Savior.

Sometimes God troubles the water through the death of someone who is very dear to us. This is an unparalleled chance to close in with God's offer of mercy. We are confronted with the loss of a friend or relative and this makes us conscious of eternity and our need of God. But sometimes we do not respond but, rather, harden our hearts and lose a good chance to get right with God.

During the Second World War many young men turned to God when they were in a foxhole. They were on the front lines; the enemy was not far away and neither was eternity. The spirit of God had troubled the waters and they made what we used to call "a foxhole decision for Christ." Now there is nothing wrong with this kind of a decision. Thousands of young men found themselves in exactly the same position—the waters were troubled during the war. But instead of responding to God, they hardened their hearts, and after a while the trouble stopped.

Certainly it is true that we can come to Christ any time we wish to do so, but there are times when the Holy Spirit moves in our lives in such a manner that it becomes easier to respond to the gospel. But if we refuse Christ at these times, it becomes increasingly more difficult to reverse our decisions. It is not that God is any less interested in us than before; the difficulty lies in the fact that our resistance builds up a hardness of heart against the movement of the Holy Spirit, making it tougher for us to break through our own hard hearts and respond.

God's Presence

When we get to the fourteenth chapter of Mark, we will deal in more detail with the beautiful story of the woman who broke the alabaster bottle of expensive perfume over Jesus' feet and head during the last week of his life on earth. When she did this, some of the disciples objected on the basis that it would have been better to have spent that money on the poor instead of wasting it in this way. Our Lord's response to this was: "Ye have the poor with you always, and whensoever you will you may do them good: but me ye have not always"(Mark 14:7).

When my grandson was three years of age, I used to drive him to nursery school. Each time we ascended or descended the stairs his little hand would go up automatically and find mine. He didn't want to fall. He had absolute confidence in the fact that I would be there. But what if I was not there? His little hand would still go up, but "Poppa" would be gone.

What most unsaved people do not realize is that God will not always be there. There are times when God is near and there are times when God is not near. I realize that this is very difficult to explain theologically, but I have lived long enough to know that it is true. The Bible gives us reason to believe this and it is echoed again and again: "Seek ye the Lord while he may be found, call ye upon him while he is near: Let the wicked forsake his way, and the unrighteous man his thoughts: and let him return unto the Lord, and he will have mercy upon him; and to our God, for he will abundantly pardon" (Isa. 55:6-7).

In many of our hymns about the Christian life we seem to realize that it is possible for us to live close to God or far away from God. We sing "Nearer My God to Thee," "Near to the Heart of God" and other similar hymns. Sometimes we talk of the *presence* of God. In other situations we use the biblical word *nigh*, etc.

Without any doubt the sinner, too, can be more aware of the presence of God at certain times in his life than he can at others. There are times when God is near and there are times when he is not near.

It seems that if we do not call upon God while he is near, there may never be another opportunity to do so. We have committed the unpardonable sin.

Before Winter

When the apostle Paul wrote to Timothy from his prison, he said, "Do thy diligence to come before winter" (2 Timothy 4:21).

Paul is writing from a Roman prison and seems to be relatively certain that it will not be long before he is executed. Timothy is one of his "sons in the faith," and Paul is very anxious to see him one more time and to have him bring some things that he had left in Troaz—a cloak, some books and some parchments.

He urges him to come "before winter" because he had personally experienced the difficulty of travelling across the Adriatic Sea to Rome at the wrong time of the year. When the Romans had attempted this with Paul as their prisoner, the vessel on which they were sailing was shipwrecked. Paul had warned them not to make the attempt at that time of the year (Acts 27). When Paul wrote to Timothy, he urged him to come before the winter winds had set in—or he might not be able to make the journey at all.

If Timothy did not come before winter, it might be too late, because by that time Paul's execution might have taken place.

At any rate, this is another passage which indicates the necessity of doing certain things when we have the opportunity lest we lose the chance. May I suggest that this is what is involved in the unpardonable sin. Sometimes we put off the problem of our salvation until it is too late. Winter has come, either by way of death or by way of lost opportunity.

There are some who have already passed the "threescore years and ten" mark in life. They have already gone beyond their prime and the grave is in view. They realize, as perhaps others in this world fail to realize, that their time is short. Others are already in the grip of some fatal disease and they know, and the doctors know, that it is only a matter of time until it is all over.

Whether we are young or old, whether we are well or gripped by disease, we are living in the "valley of the shadow of death." We are journeying through that sphere of time, which God has cut out of eternity, in which death has jurisdiction and at any moment may claim us as his victim.

Someday we must die. It could be anytime. It might be today. The only time that really belongs to us is the immediate present. Next year belongs to God. Next month belongs to God. Tomorrow belongs to God. The next hour of our lives belongs to God. The only time that is ours is now. The only time that we can make decisions is now. The only time during which we can accept Christ is now. We control the "now" of our lives. God controls the future.

That is why the Bible says, "Behold, now is the accepted time; behold, now is the day of salvation" (2 Cor. 6:2). That is why God warns: "Boast not thyself of tomorrow; for thou knowest not what a day may bring forth" (Prov. 27:1). In this age of war, accidents and sudden death we might well read that verse: Boast not thyself of *the next hour*, for thou knowest not what a *moment* may bring forth.

If we fail to accept Jesus Christ as our Savior now, there may be no tomorrow. Once death has claimed us as his victim, our chance to get right with God will be gone.

However, even if death is not about to claim us, we may lose our opportunity to accept Jesus Christ as our Savior—simply because we have rejected him too long. Almost every evangelist, pastor and Christian worker can recall cases of men and women who had many opportunities to accept the Lord Jesus Christ but continually rejected him and finally seemed to arrive at the place in their lives where it became impossible for them to respond.

Here is what happens. The first time a person hears the gospel, his heart is strangely stirred. There is a pungent spirit of conviction that moves him God-ward. The Spirit of God is wooing him towards the Lord Jesus Christ. Everything within him seems to be urging him to accept the divine invitation. It would be the easiest thing in the world for him to do so, but for some reason, that first time he resists the convicting power of the Spirit of God, and although it is a struggle for him to do so, he says his first no to Jesus Christ. It is hard to reject; it would have been easy to accept.

The next time he hears the gospel, again there is a great spirit of conviction upon him. Again the Spirit of God is working in his life. Again everything within him seems to urge him to respond. Again it would be easy to close in with God, but again he yields to the dictates of Satan within his life, and says, "no." But now it is a little easier to reject and it has become a little more difficult to accept.

Again and again he hears the gospel. There is again the struggle of the soul. The Spirit of God convicts. Satan draws the other way. But down through the years he refuses to reverse his decision until now it has become difficult to say no, and it is growing increasingly difficult to say yes. It is a simple matter now to resist the working of the Spirit, and it would be difficult for him to yield.

As long as a person continues to resist the working of the Spirit of God, he is building up a wall of resistance around his own heart that will eventually become so strong and so callous that it will be impossible for him to change. When that day comes, he will have said no for the last time, and never again will he say yes.

I do not believe that the Spirit of God draws a deadline in the life of any person, but I am thoroughly convinced that a man may draw the deadline for himself by a continual rejection of the Lord Jesus Christ.

"But," you say, "how do I know but that already I have said my final no to God? Maybe I have already drawn the deadline of opportunity across my life. It could be that my heart has become so hard and callous and indifferent to the pleading of the Spirit of God that it would be impossible for me to relent and turn to God even now. How can I tell when the deadline has been drawn?"

In other words, how do I know that I have not already committed the unpardonable sin? Is your heart stirred? Is there any interest at all? Is there the least evidence of the convicting power of the Spirit of God? Are you concerned in any way about your soul's salvation? If so, then you have not crossed the deadline. As long as there is interest, as long as there is concern, as long as there is any sign of anxiety whatsoever, you have not committed the unpardonable sin.

But let us remember, there is a day of harvest, but there is a day when the harvest ends. There is a summertime of opportunity, but there is a time when the summer will be past. God grant that we may respond when the Spirit of God troubles the waters, that we may call upon God while he is near, and that we may "come before winter."

Part Two

The Farmer and the Soil — Chapter 4
The Woman and the Tassel — Chapter 5
The Boy and the Lunch — Chapter 6

Hearken; Behold, there went out a sower to sow: And it came to pass, as he sowed, some fell by the way side, and the fowls of the air came and devoured it up. And some fell on stony ground, where it had not much earth; and immediately it sprang up, because it had no depth of earth: But when the sun was up, it was scorched; and because it had no root, it withered away. And some fell among thorns, and the thorns grew up, and choked it, and it yielded no fruit. And other fell on good ground, and did yield fruit that sprang up and increased; and brought forth, some thirty, and some sixty, and some an hundred. And he said unto them, "He that hath ears to hear, let him hear."

Mark 4:3-9

Chapter 4

The Farmer and the Soil

This was the point in our Lord's ministry when he was extremely popular. He was attracting huge crowds. The people followed him everywhere he went. In this fourth chapter of the gospel of Mark the crowd is so large that he stepped into a small boat, pushed it away from the shore and talked to the people who were standing on the banks.

Perhaps today we would call this "church growth." But in the midst of all of this apparent success and excitement Jesus tells a rather sad story. He had been preaching and teaching the people almost without a break, but apparently a great deal of what he was saying was making very little impact upon them. I am sure Jesus was very much interested in the number of people to whom he was talking. As we noted earlier in this book, our Lord dealt continually with huge crowds of people. He did not minister to only a select few. However, Jesus realized that there was another statistic that was more important than the number of bodies that were there to hear the Word. He was much more concerned about how much of the Word reached the hearts of these people and made a difference in their lives.

No matter who teaches, preaches or writes the Word of God, that person will be violently opposed by Satan. Jesus mentions three ways that Satan can make the sowing of the seed worth very little or absolutely nothing. He describes them as birds, rocks and thorns.

The Birds

"And it came to pass, as he sowed, some fell by the wayside, and the fowls of the air came and devoured it up" (Mark 4:4).

This is seed that doesn't even get well started. The moment it is thrown out, the birds dive down, pluck it up, and carry it away. Every Sunday morning in a thousand churches the devil has his birds poised and ready to dive the moment the seed is sown. There are several different kinds of birds that prevent the seed from taking root in a church service. One of these would be the interruptions—a baby crying, people talking, someone fainting. It doesn't take very much to distract most of us. It is imperative that we find out whose baby is crying and why they do not take it out.

There are young people in the row behind us who insist on talking about what they were doing the night before, and of course it is essential that we turn around and give them one of those pious looks that says, "How dare you!"

It is certainly unfortunate if someone faints, but surely the people sitting close by can handle it while the rest of us concentrate a little more diligently on hearing the Word of God. But no, most of the congregation is totally distracted until the person is finally carried out. The "interruption" bird has done its job and the devil has been successful in seeing that a lot of the seed has been wasted.

Another rather innocent-looking bird that is ready to dive the moment the preacher begins to speak is "drowsiness." Most of the important social functions in this world take place on Saturday night—because, for the devil's crowd, Sunday is a chance to sleep in. Unfortunately, many of God's people get caught in the Saturday night syndrome, and although we do not sleep in on Sunday morning, we do become extremely drowsy. And, of course, the moment our head begins to nod, the devil has been victorious. The bird of "drowsiness" has done his work and a great deal more of the seed does not take root.

The third bird that is poised for the devil's duty on Sunday morning is the bird of "wandering thoughts." A good Christian boy sees a beautiful Christian girl on the other side of the auditorium and instead of listening to the Word, he allows himself to float out into a cloud of sexual fantasies. The businessman begins thinking about Monday—the board meeting, the sales program, the business appointment, etc. Many good business plans are developed between eleven and twelve o'clock on Sunday morning—a time that was supposed to have been devoted to hearing the Word of God.

Of course, by about twenty minutes before twelve, a great many people have stopped listening to the sermon and are beginning to think about lunch—with whom, in what restaurant, what sort of food, and so on. The bird of "wandering thoughts" has done his duty for the devil.

Many of these same birds attack us in our personal devotional lives. Many of us have never learned how to wage the war of Bible study and prayer. Our personal time of devotion is not just a nice religious habit. It is a time when we are engaging the devil and he is going to do everything within his power to send his birds in to destroy the effectiveness of our warfare.

The apostle Paul was certainly aware of this struggle when he said, "For we wrestle not against flesh and blood, but against principalities, against powers, against the rulers of the darkness of this world, against spiritual wickedness in high places" (Eph. 6:12). In this passage the praying doesn't start until the spiritual armor has been put on.

Israel was born in this kind of personal struggle: "And Jacob was left alone; and there wrestled a man with him until the breaking of the day." When his opponent was about to pull away and leave him, Jacob cried out in desperation, "I will not let thee go, accept thou bless me" (Gen. 32:24,26).

It was as a result of this struggle that God changed Jacob's name to Israel, but it did not happen easily. There was a battle, a struggle, a warfare.

Moses was familiar with this spiritual warfare. After the people had bowed before the golden calf and worshipped it in the wilderness, Moses went back up into the mountain to confront God. Can you catch some of the desperate struggle there must have been when he cried out to God, "If thou wilt forgive their sin—; and if not, blot me, I pray thee, out of thy book which thou hast written" (Exod. 32:32).

Samuel's mother was no stranger to this warfare. It seemed that it was impossible for her to bear children, and perhaps more than anything else in life she wanted to have a son. We can hear the struggle of her soul when she went up to the temple to pray. Listen to it: "O Lord of hosts, if thou wilt indeed look on the affliction of thine handmaid, and remember me, and not forget thine handmaid, but wilt give unto thine handmaid a man child, then I will give him unto the Lord all the days of his life, and there shall no razor come upon his head" (1 Sam. 1:11).

And, of course, the result of that spiritual battle was the great prophet Samuel, whom God was going to use in such a mighty way in the life of King David.

I think that we have forgotten that the Christian is a soldier. He is in an army. There is a war to be waged. There is a battle to be won. There is a strong enemy—and unless we learn how to engage in this spiritual warfare, we will be defeated.

I have named only three of the birds that are used by the devil to carry away the seed of God's Word so that it does not have the effect that it could have—interruptions, drowsiness, and wandering thoughts. But the devil has a thousand other birds, and we need to realize that they will dive in and do everything within their power to make the Word of God useless.

The Rocks

"And some fell on stony ground, where it had not much earth; and immediately it sprang up, because it had no depth of earth: But when the sun was up, it was scorched; and because it had no root, it withered away" (Mark 4:5-6).

The rocks might represent people who go to church for the wrong reasons and therefore come out having had some shallow kind of emotional experience. How often I have heard people describing the blessing of a service in words like these: "I felt so warm! What an experience that was! Oh, the fantastic music, the beautiful lights, the scenery!" These were the things these people expected to get in church. They got exactly what they expected, and no more.

Most Christians can manage somehow to struggle to church on Sunday morning. But whether they come back, or not, to the evening service depends upon some rather strange things. What's on tonight? Is the music from one of those loud groups? Or is it going to be done by somebody who is rather straight? What is the preacher like? Is he funny, dramatic, brief, good-looking . . . ?

Of course, people who ask these kinds of questions will not be fed very much spiritually, because no matter how effectively the Word is preached or sung, it is doomed to fall on shallow ground because these are shallow Christians. Their experience with Christ is tied to a few catch phrases. The politician is said to be Christian if he says "God" three or four times in his speech. Very few self-respecting people would not admit that they are "born again." They may not be quite sure what that means, but they think it is a good club to which to belong. When asked about their Christian faith, some people answer that they attend an evangelical church. In many cases there has been no change, there has been no cross, there has been no revolution.

Christianity starts with a great conviction of sin—without Jesus I am a no-good, a nothing, a doomed man. I am totally lost, bound, blind and dead. I need forgiveness. I wish liberation. I need life. Call it a "guilt trip" if you wish, but this sort of thing is in the Bible from cover to cover.

Sad to say, much of the Word of God that is sown today falls on extremely shallow ground. The shallow ground of emotion. The shallow ground of excitement. The shallow ground of crowds. The shallow ground of music. The shallow ground of friendship. The shallow ground of social contact. The seed is sown, but it hasn't got a chance. It falls on shallow ground—that bit of ground that lies on top of the rocks.

The Thorns

"And some fell among thorns, and the thorns grew up, and choked it, and it yielded no fruit" (Mark 4:7).

Jesus mentions three forms that these thorns may take—the cares of this world, the deceitfulness of riches, and the lust of other things.

Some people live in a home where Christianity is not welcomed. Others work at a job where being a good Christian is almost impossible. There is nothing wrong with either of these situations, as long as we are prepared to fight the battle that is involved in giving the Word of God first place in our lives despite the cares of the world.

There is nothing wrong with wealth. I don't think the Bible ever states that it is a wicked thing to be wealthy. However, where the source of our wealth is dishonest or the methods of accumulating it are unethical, then we are confronted with one of the thorns in this life that can prevent the seed from growing.

Sometimes the source of our riches is quite alright and the methods are excellent, but we get involved in a task that consumes all of our time. There is no time left for the Word of God. How many people there are in every church who should sing in the choir, but they haven't got time. In a church that has home Bible fellowships almost everybody in the church says, "I should go to a home Bible fellowship—but I haven't got the time."

These are people who are not doing a bad thing, but they have allowed themselves to get involved in making money in a task which demands too much of their time. That is the point at which riches becomes one of the thorns that the devil uses to choke out the Word.

The third kind of thorns that Jesus mentions is called "the lust of other things." Sometimes the desire for other things involves activity that violates the principles of the Bible. Of course, these are wrong and must be terminated if the seed is to find root in our lives. But more often the desire for other things involves activity that, like the accumulation of wealth, consumes time that should be given to God. The devil uses the pursuit of these activities as thorns to choke out the Word of God.

Many people make a big thing out of what they call their "intellectual doubts." If somebody would just explain it to me . . . . But what about so and so? Is there an answer to this question? In my experience there are very few people who have honest intellectual doubts. Usually this is just a smoke screen to cover up the thorns. How much better it would be to admit: "I have thorns in my life that are choking out the Word of God, and I must do something about them."

Conclusion

When I study this interesting story of the sower and the seed, I generally have a tendency to ask the question "Which kind of soil am I?"

I think this is the wrong question to ask. In all probability each of us can potentially be all four kinds of soil. There are times when we are the "wayside path," and the birds take away the seed. There are other times when we are the rocky ground, and the seed only has a shallow area in which to work. Sometimes we are the thorny area, and the effectiveness of the Word of God is continually being choked out by the thorns.

Fortunately, all of us have the potential of being good ground. We can bring forth plentifully. Jesus is careful to point out the fact that all will not produce in the same quantities. Some will be thirty-fold, some sixty, and some a hundred. Let us make every effort to protect the seed from the birds, to break up the stony ground that is preventing it from developing firm roots and to eliminate the thorns whenever we see them. Then we can be good ground.

And a certain woman, which had an issue of blood twelve years, and had suffered many things of many physicians, and had spent all that she had, and was nothing bettered, but rather grew worse, when she had heard of Jesus, came in the press behind, and touched his garment. For she said, "If I may touch but his clothes, I shall be whole." And straightway the fountain of her blood was dried up; and she felt in her body that she was healed of that plague.

Mark 5:25-29

Chapter 5

The Woman and the Tassel

In his fourth chapter Mark tells three miraculous stories. The first is the story of the Gadarene demoniac out of whom Jesus cast a legion of devils. This was the time that he allowed the devils to enter a herd of swine, who promptly ran down a steep hill into the sea. Three thousand of them were drowned.

Then Mark tells two interwoven stores. A ruler of the synagogue by the name of Jairus came to Jesus and urged him to come and heal his daughter, whom he said was at the point of death. While Jesus was making his way through the usual enormous crowd, Mark interjects the story of the woman with the issue of blood, who touched the hem of our Lord's garment and was healed.

There was an early Christian legend that this woman's name was Veronica. So let's use that name so that she becomes a little more realistic to us. In addition to using this name, I would like us to use our imaginations a little more and connect Veronica with Jairus and his wife and his

49

daughter. It might have happened this way:

It all took place in an Eastern city many years ago. The downtowns of the East are always crowded—not like downtown Toronto, or Chicago, or Detroit, with our huge buildings towering into blue skies, or falling rain, or grey smoke; with our beautiful stores set in orderly fashion along straight streets, usually laid out in perfect squares; with our big crowds of business people and shoppers, all dressed very nearly the same as the next person, pushing their way along the sidewalks in accordance with modern traffic regulations.

There is no order in most Eastern cities. Sometimes the streets are exceptionally wide, like the main street of Calcutta with its conglomeration of street cars, automobiles, horsedrawn coaches, rickshaws, sacred cattle and countless people. Sometimes the streets are only wide enough for two rickshaws to pass one another. There is the usual line of buildings and shops where business is carried on inside, but in the East the salesmen believe in going out where the people are. Every store takes advantage of the sidewalk space in front to display its wares. Small-time businessmen and women who cannot afford a building simply establish themselves and their shops wherever they can find space on the sidewalk or on the street. There is no such thing as walking straight down the street.

The huge crowds of noisy, gesticulating, colorfully dressed people wind very slowly in and out around the sidewalk stalls. On the streets there is a constant blowing of horns, screeching of brakes and clanging of streetcar bells. Take away the modern means of transport and you have a picture of the town through which Jesus was making his way to heal the twelve-year-old daughter of Jairus.

There would have been a crowd around Jesus. There always was. But on this particular day, with this unusual attraction, the crowd would have been much larger, and concentrated in one area. Jesus must have been in the center, then the disciples, struggling to stay as close as possible. Then came those who were vitally interested in seeing him because they loved him, or because they hated him, or because they were curious. Then there were also those who were jostling along in the fringe of the crowd, not for any special reason except that there was a crowd. Finally, there would be the normal Eastern multitude, many of them aggravated because the progress of their business had been interrupted.

The story centers around a woman—a woman that had once been a tiny baby, warm and clean and healthy in her mother's arms, untouched by the sin and disease of the world. A woman that had been a little girl playing in the streets with her friends—happy, carefree, with the wonder

50

of life before her. A woman whose pathway had been crossed by the onslaught of a dreadful disease—a disease that had lined her face and greyed her hair and bent her back and crippled her limbs and wasted her body. A disease that had put the light out of her eyes, wiped the smile off her lips, ripped the joy from her heart. A disease that had warped her mind, damaged her soul and was about to finally destroy her body. She had tried everything and everybody. She had reached the end of her hope, the end of her patience, the end of her resources. This is the way she came to Jesus. She had nothing to lose. In her exhausted, hopeless state, she might as well make one more attempt.

Perhaps she argued with herself—shall I, or shall I not? Maybe I could speak to him. No, there are too many people. Maybe I could do something to attract his attention and he would look at me. No, I might not be successful. Maybe I could reach one of his disciples. No, that would not be enough.

Suddenly the thought struck her: If I could but touch the hem of his garment. That's it. I won't bother him. I won't try to talk to him. I won't even attract his attention. I'll simply squeeze through the crowd and touch him. Possessed of this thought, she began to move.

Now let's move our story back twelve years. At that time Veronica had been a young woman on the domestic staff of a prominent Jewish man named Jairus, whom the Bible describes as one of the rulers of the synagogue. Jairus would have been the man who arranged the synagogue services. He would decide who of the men would pray, who would read the Law, who would read the Prophets and who would preach. He was probably quite wealthy and certainly a very important man in his community.

Veronica joined his staff when she was eighteen years of age. Her main task was to be a personal assistant to Jairus's wife. She was well paid for what she did and was able to save a considerable amount of money.

Now let us go back to the crowded street where Jesus was still making his way through the throng while the woman was still pushing closer and closer to him. She paused for a moment and looked at the people around her. She could see Jesus not very far away from her now. She had heard so much about him. They said he was kind. He was sympathetic. He was patient. He was wise. But they also said that he had power—power to discern men's thoughts, power to heal the sick, power to raise the dead. He had the power of God.

In this account we see her in the right crowd. These people had come to see the healing of a rich man's daughter. This crowd was with Jesus.

Certainly this was the right place to be. She was not in the sports arena watching the bloody spectacles of the day. She was not in the gambling den mingling with the backwash of society. She was not in the tavern trying to drown her sorrow and pain in alcohol. She was in the right crowd. . . .

As she paused for a moment to rest, she thought back once more to those early days in the home of Jairus.

The Jairus family had been expecting their first baby. She remembered it well. She had herself arranged for the midwife to be there on time, but the baby came five weeks early. How well she remembered the consternation and excitement when Jairus's wife realized that she was not going to be assisted by the midwife. Veronica did everything within her power to help. Although she had never delivered a baby before, she had seen it done on several occasions. The birth seemed to take forever, but finally there was that first little cry. The baby was there and in its mother's arms.

Veronica left the room and went upstairs to her own little room where she sat down, totally exhausted. Suddenly there was an excruciating pain in the lower part of her stomach. Before she knew what was happening she began to hemorrhage. It went on and on and on. She went to one doctor after another. She tried remedy after remedy. Finally, the little amount of money that she had been able to save was gone. She had an incurable disease, and furthermore, a disease that had made it impossible for her to associate with normal people. She was an outcast.

And now, twelve years later, as she sat there resting, hoping to gain sufficient strength to get over to Jesus, she thought about her situation. She was bankrupt. She had spent all of her money on doctors and remedies, and she was still very weak from a continual loss of blood. She was an outcast of Jewish society: she was not supposed to touch anybody; she could not participate in synagogue or temple services; she was ceremonially unclean—shut off from worship of any kind. In other words, she was alive, but that was all. Certainly she had nothing to lose.

Isn't this so often the case with us. We try everything else first, and then we turn to God. When we are young and strong and healthy we spend our time with other people. Then at last, when we are more or less shipwrecked, we turn to God. The hymnwriter said it so well:

> Abide with me; fast falls the even-tide,
> The darkness deepens; Lord, with me abide.
> When other helpers fail and comforts flee,
> Help of the helpless, O abide with me.

William Kirkpatrick, (1838-1921), the Methodist hymn writer who had been a Fife major during the Civil War and then a furniture dealer in Philadelphia, puts it succinctly:

I wasted many precious years,
Now I'm coming home;
I now repent with bitter tears,
Lord, I'm coming home.

Of course, this was probably the very first time she had ever been near Jesus, and the wonderful thing about Veronica was the fact that she took advantage of it in spite of her misgivings and physical weakness. The baby that she had delivered in the home of Jairus twelve years ago was dying—she might already be dead—and Jesus would have to keep moving in order to get there in time. But then she was dying, too, and with this thought in her mind, she decided to make a final, desperate attempt. She reached for that last little bit of strength as slowly she struggled on.

It was difficult. She was very weak, and the pressure of the crowd was almost impossible. But there he was, almost within reach—another yard—another foot—just one inch. The hem of his robe was within sight. When she saw his robe she remembered that that was the kind of robe that she had been responsible to take care of for Jairus. She looked for the little blue tassels that she knew would be hanging down low at the four corners. With her last little bit of strength she reached out and touched that tassel on Jesus' robe.

She felt the cloth, and then it was gone. He had passed by. But no. He had not passed by. He had stopped. Jesus had stopped. The touch of this emaciated, hopeless, disillusioned, broken-hearted woman had stopped God.

She had no money. She did not meet him in a house of worship. She met him on the street. She had no private audience with the Lord. She touched him in a crowd. She touched him in faith—in desperate, believing faith; and he stopped. The touch of one anonymous woman in a crowd halted the Lord of glory. He who conquered death. He who defeated Satan. He whom all the legions of hell cannot stop. He who is King of Kings. He stopped, just because a sick woman named Veronica had touched the tassel on his robe.

The miracle was instantaneous. What the doctors had not been able to do, Jesus did. What her money could not buy, Jesus gave her. Her need was met. Her burden was lifted. Her problem was solved. Her body was healed. And her life was changed.

It is difficult to help others without sacrificing something ourselves. "And Jesus, immediately knowing in himself that virtue had gone out of him, turned him about in the press, and said, 'Who touched my clothes?' " (Mark 5:30). If it cost Jesus something to be of help to this woman, how much more should you and I expect that we may have to suffer if we are really going to be of any good to others.

Almost every preacher of the gospel knows this: that if he goes into the pulpit with a burden for his people and he unloads that burden, it drains him immensely. There is a sense in which a little bit of the preacher should die every time he preaches effectively. That is one reason why many preachers have great difficulty in making small talk at the close of a service in which they have really unburdened their hearts.

The second lesson that we should learn is that there was no magic power in the little blue tassel that hung from the corner of Jesus' robe. As far as Veronica was concerned, she may have thought there was, but Jesus corrected that thought immediately when he said to her, "Daughter, thy faith has made thee whole" (Mark 5:34).

There was no magic about it. What performed the miracle was the power of God combined with the faith of this woman.

It is of vital importance that we do not depend upon the "tassels" of our religion to perform miracles in our lives. It is not the image that stands in the corner. It is not the cross that hangs on the wall. It is not the relics or remains or holy ground. It is not baptism, communion or mass. It is the power of God which responds to our faith. That's what creates a spiritual miracle of any kind. It is not magic, but God.

That day, this woman, Veronica, joined the great army of people who have come into personal contact with the Son of God—those who have reached through the crowd with the arm of faith and touched him. Those whose lives have been transformed because they touched him. Whose sins have been washed away because they touched him. Whose purpose in life has been changed because they touched him, whose hearts have been softened, whose minds have been purified, whose actions have been cleaned up, whose dispositions have been sweetened, whose souls have been stirred because they touched him.

Many years ago when I preached on the story of this woman who touched the tassel of our Lord's robe my sister, Hope Evangeline, was inspired to write this beautiful poem which she entitled, simply, "The Hem of His Garment."

She once had the bloom of youth in her cheek,
  Her hair was like threads of pure gold;
Her beautiful eyes once sparkled so bright,
  But sickness had made her grow old.

Her face had become so wrinkled and worn,
  The gold in her hair had turned grey;
The light in her eyes had vanished and left
  A look of despair and dismay.

It seemed that no one could help her or find
  The cause of her suffering and pain;
Hopeless, forsaken, she trudged on her way,
  From weeping she could not refrain.

Just then thro' her tears she looked and behold,
  The face of the Master appeared;
His eyes were filled with compassion and love,
  At last she had found One who cared.

Wending her way thro' the crowds to his side,
  There humbly before him she kneeled;
She touched the hem of his garment and lo,
  All at once she knew she was healed.

If you have wandered away from his side
  And tears now your pathway obscure,
Just look thro' your tears like the woman of old,
  There's nothing that he cannot cure.

The third lesson that we should learn from this story is that a public confession is usually demanded by Jesus. Veronica had every reason to remain a secret believer. In those days women were not supposed to talk very much on the public street. In addition to this, her particular problem was an embarrassment that no woman would want to discuss.

However, Jesus insisted that she identify herself. He demanded a public testimony. Maybe he asked for this so that it would be made clear right at the beginning that she could now be accepted by other people even though she had been an outcast for so long. Or he may have asked her to do it so that her other "outcast" friends would realize that there was a difference and would not expect her to spend much of her time with them in the future.

This may be one of the reasons for a public confession of any kind. It determines with which group of people we are going to mingle, and it makes it clear to our old friends in the world that we have now joined another group.

In the Old Testament the psalmist put it this way, "Call upon me in the day of trouble: I will deliver thee, and thou shalt glorify me" (Psalm 50:15). After we have been delivered by God he expects us to glorify him—to make a public confession.

The classic passage is in the book of Romans: "That if thou shalt confess with thy mouth the Lord Jesus, and shalt believe in thine heart that God has raised him from the dead, thou shalt be saved. For with the heart man believeth unto righteousness; and with the mouth confession is made unto salvation" (Romans 10:9-10).

Nearly two thousand years ago a sick woman was so desperate that she pushed through a great crowd and touched one of the tassels of Jesus' garment. God stopped. And she was transformed.

God has led you to read this chapter for a purpose. He is here to help you. He is waiting for you to touch him. You can stop God. And when he stops, you will never be the same again.

And they departed into a desert place by ship privately. And the people saw them departing, and many knew him, and ran afoot thither out of all cities, and outwent them, and came together unto him. And Jesus, when he came out, saw much people, and was moved with compassion toward them, because they were as sheep not having a shepherd: and he began to teach them many things. And when the day was now far spent, his disciples came unto him, and said, "This is a desert place, and now the time is far passed: Send them away, that they may go into the country round about, and into the villages, and buy themselves bread: for they have nothing to eat." He answered and said unto them, "Give ye them to eat." And they say unto him, "Shall we go and buy two hundred pennyworth of bread, and give them to eat?"

Mark 6: 32 - 37

Chapter 6

The Boy and the Lunch

John the Baptist was dead. At the request of his wife, Herodias, King Herod had chopped off his head and presented it to his daughter on a silver platter. Herodias hated John because he stood before the king and said, "It is not lawful for thee to have thy brother's wife" (Mark 6:10).

But now Herod was beginning to hear stories about Jesus. He thought that John the Baptist had risen from the dead and had come back to haunt him. Not only was Jesus performing miracles himself, but he had sent his disciples all over the country, two by two, and he had given them power to cast out devils and heal the sick. It was springtime in Palestine and the grass was green. In John's account he mentions the fact that it was the time of the Passover—which would account for the green grass. In all probability it was the middle of April in the year A.D. 29.

The disciples had just come back from their strenuous preaching mission. During their absence Jesus had been busy teaching in the villages near his home town, Nazareth, but he had not been able to heal very many because to them he was nothing more than a carpenter with whom they had grown up. As Jesus said, "A prophet is not without honour, but in his own country, and among his own kin, and in his own house" (Mark 6:4). Their unbelief had made it impossible for him to perform many miracles.

Although some of the people had become hostile to him, there was still a large crowd that followed him everywhere he went. At this time the crowds were much larger than normal. In addition to the people who lived in Nazareth and Capernaum and other villages around the sea of Galilee, there were thousands of devout Jewish pilgrims on their way to Jerusalem to celebrate the Passover. When the disciples returned from their preaching mission, Jesus knew that they would need some rest. It had been a very strenuous period for them. They had taken no baggage with them—not even a bag, or bread, or money, or change of clothes. And in this "no baggage" condition they would have been able to cover a lot of ground. With that rapid movement from village to village they had used up a great deal of strength and energy. They were very tired.

After they had given Jesus a report of their ministry, he suggested that they leave the festive crowds, go across the Sea of Galilee in a boat to a place where they could be by themselves and rest. It was a four-mile journey across the lake.

A huge crowd of people decided that they would follow Jesus and the disciples to the other side, but they had to go on foot—around the north end of the lake—a distance of about ten miles. The crowd was massed at the shore when Jesus and the disciples landed.

Let me give you an idea of what this crowd had accomplished. The Peoples Church is located in the north end of the city of Toronto, about ten miles north of Lake Ontario. The church seats approximately two thousand people. Imagine that we are to pack it full three times, and after each service empty the crowd out onto Sheppard Avenue. Suddenly somebody says, "Let's go to the Toronto harbour!" So the six thousand people move quickly by foot a distance of ten miles.

That is approximately what this crowd in Jesus' day had done. By the time the boat with Jesus and his disciples in it had crossed the lake—a distance of only four miles—the crowd had walked rapidly or perhaps even run around the north end of the lake. They were there to greet Jesus and the disciples on their arrival. Jesus got out of the boat and immediately began teaching them. He continued until about three o'clock in the afternoon, at which time he decided to feed them.

He asked the disciples to organize the crowd into groups of fifty and one hundred. This may have been done in columns or rows, making fifty rows of one hundred people in each. But it is more likely that the disciples arranged them in the form of a great outdoors banquet hall. There would have been fifty people at each table and one hundred "tables" consisting of the grass upon which the people were sitting. In addition to these people, there were also some women and children—say, one thousand women and their children, requiring at least twenty more tables.

The people were in a festive mood—not sitting up, but reclining as if they were about to have a party, a celebration or a feast. A little boy had given Jesus his lunch, which consisted of two small dried fish and five pieces of bread made out of barley. Barley loaves were the food of poor people. If these people had been wealthy they would have had bread made out of wheat flour. Our Lord took the bread, lifted it up to God and blessed it with one of the typical Jewish blessings: "Praise unto thee, Oh Lord, our God, King of the world; who causeth bread to come forth from the earth."

Then Jesus gave each of the disciples a small amount of the food—enough to fill his basket. (When they were travelling away from home, most Jews carried with them a small basket in which they put their kosher food. This enabled them to move about the country not dependent upon buying food from the shops, nor on eating food that was not ceremonially clean.)

After the disciples had served each of the more than one hundred table groups, they picked up what had been left over. When they came back to where Jesus was waiting for them, each of their baskets was still full so that they could sit down with Jesus and eat their own supper. This story tells us at least three things:

1. *Jesus rewards people who put forth a great deal of effort in order to follow him.*

Our Lord began to teach them the moment his foot hit the shore. Although he must have been extremely tired himself, he rewarded the effort that they had made. He taught them. They had been blessed by our Lord's words because they had been hungry enough to put forth an effort to hear him.

It is just the same today. If we want to know and understand the Bible, we must be willing to make an effort to do so. But when we do, God promises to satisfy our hunger: "Blessed are they which do hunger and thirst after righteousness: for they shall be filled" (Matt. 5:6).

The psalmist understood this spiritual principal: "As the hart panteth after the water brooks, so panteth my soul after thee, oh God. My soul thirsteth for God, for the living God: My soul longeth, yea, even fainteth for the courts of the Lord: my heart and my flesh crieth out for the living God" (Ps. 42:1-2, 84:2).

Most Christians put forth whatever effort may be necessary to go to church on Sunday morning. Moreover, they are active in the work of their church. Some of them teach in the Sunday school, others work as ushers, some sing in the choir, some look after the public address system, and so on. But a great many of these "faithful" Sunday morning Christians never dream of coming back to the church again on Sunday night. There are so many lovely things that can be done on Sunday night. The possibilities are tremendous. Should we spend Sunday evening relaxing with the family around a hot meal? Or should we spend Sunday evening reclining with the family before the television set? Or perhaps we should spend Sunday evening going to bed early so that we will be fresh for our work the next day? Or in some parts of the country we could spend Sunday evening sitting around the pool in the beautiful weather?

Or should we go to church on Sunday night and listen to the teaching of the Word of God? I think the sad fact is that many modern Christians don't even ask these questions. Spending Sunday night in church is not even considered. It is not one of the options. The thought never goes through their minds. But, you say, can I not be a Christian without going to church on Sunday night? Of course you can but it's like:

> A student who won't go to school—
> A soldier who won't join the army—
> A citizen who doesn't pay taxes and doesn't vote—
> A salesman with no customers—
> A seaman on a ship without a crew—
> A businessman on a deserted island—
> An author without readers—
> A tuba player without an orchestra—
> A parent without a family—
> A football player without a team—
> A politician who is a hermit—
> A bee without a hive.

Sad to say, there is very little real hunger for the Word of God among our people today. The prophet Amos says a terrible word about the absence of hunger for the Word of God: "Behold, the days come, sayeth the Lord God, that I will send a famine in the land, not a famine of bread, nor a thirst for water, but of hearing the words of the Lord" (Amos 8:11).

When I visited Russia in 1958, the only churches I could see without any effort were Orthodox cathedrals that were at that time used for other purposes. The one Protestant church was on a side street, and I had to get a taxi and ask him to take me to it. There was a famine of churches in Russia. And a parallel famine of the Word of God.

In 1983 I visited China. When I was there, I saw no churches, but I was successful in getting some literature across the border and into the hands of one of the pastors of an underground church—one of the "house churches" of China. I took in Bibles, hymnbooks and a number of copies of *Streams in the Desert*—second only to the Bible among Christians in China.

At 11:30 on a dark night—there are few streetlights and what cars there are use only their parking lights—I realized I was in the midst of a famine for the Word of God. The pastor's daughter came out of the darkness to get the literature from our taxi. She did so at great personal peril.

The apostle Peter said, "As newborn babes, desire the sincere milk of the word, that ye may grow thereby" (1 Pet. 2:2).

Paul adds, "Study to show thyself approved unto God, a workman that needeth not to be ashamed, rightly dividing the word of truth" (2 Tim. 2:15).

Most of us have more Bibles than we can use. They are on our library shelves, our coffee tables, and sometimes even on the dashboards of our cars. We have a great surplus of Bibles—in a world where many people cannot even come into possession of a single copy of one part of the Bible.

Not only do we have Bibles, but we also have access to wonderful pastors who know how to teach us what the Bible says. There may be three or four meetings during a given week in most churches during which we can hear the Word of God. But in most cases we make it out to the great "celebration" on Sunday morning, and that is the last of our Bible study for that week.

In addition to all of the study my father did all of his life, he observed the habit of starting at the first word of the first chapter of Genesis and reading the Bible from beginning to end. When he got to the last verse of the book of Revelation he would go back and start once again with Genesis. I do not know how many times he read the Bible completely. I don't think he knew himself, but he lived for ninety-six years. He was converted when he was sixteen, and that gave him a lot of time to absorb the Word of God.

I wonder if we have ever realized how long it takes to read the Bible. If we were to read at the rather formal rate that the pastor uses in the pulpit on Sunday morning, it would take us seventy hours and forty minutes to read the entire Bible. It would take us fifty-two hours and twenty minutes to read the Old Testament, eighteen hours and twenty minutes to read the New Testament. In the Old Testament the Book of Psalms takes the longest—four hours and twenty-eight minutes. In the New Testament, the Gospel of Luke takes the longest—two hours and forty-three minutes.

2. If we give away what we have in our baskets, God will refill them.

The disciples were just as hungry as the people—perhaps even hungrier, because they had just come back from that arduous preaching mission. It would have been a great temptation for them to have eaten their own share first and then after they were well filled to have fed the crowd.

That is what most churches do with their spiritual food. We have a tendency to look after ourselves first; then, if there is anything left, we will reach out to the rest of the world. After we get our sanctuary erected, after we get the new educational wing built, after we have constructed the new chapel, after this and after that—then we will do something about the need of the world for the gospel. It has been my experience that churches who say this never do get to the end of their building program. As soon as one building is finished, they begin planning another. And so it is that we look after ourselves while the rest of the world goes to hell.

We seem to have completely forgotten the biblical principle of giving: "Give, and it shall be given unto you; good measure, pressed down, and shaken together, and running over, shall men give into your bosom. For with the same measure that ye mete withal it shall be measured to you again" (Luke 6:38).

"He that findeth his life shall lose it; and he that loseth his life for my sake shall find it" (Matt. 10:39).

"Except a corn of wheat fall into the ground and die, it abideth alone; but if it die, it bringeth for much fruit" (John 12:24).

But this principle is not limited to the New Testament. There is a wonderful story that expresses the same concept in the Old Testament. It's the beautiful story of the prophet Elijah and the widow of

Zarephath. Elijah had caused the rain in his country to stop so that the land was gradually drying up. God told him to go to the brook Cherith, and there God commanded the ravens to feed him. When that brook dried up, God told Elijah to go to Zarephath, where he would find a widow who would look after him.

Sure enough, when he got to the gate of that city, the woman was there gathering sticks. Elijah asked her to give him a little water to drink.

As she was going to get the water, he called after her, "Bring me, I pray thee, a morsel of bread in thine hand." The widow turned to Elijah in desperation and said that she did not have any bread, only a little bit of meal in a barrel and a small amount of oil in a bottle. She said she was gathering the sticks to make a fire and fix the last bit of food they had. She and her son would then eat it and die. But Elijah was insistent. He asked the woman to give him a piece of bread first and then to feed herself and her son. However, he added that if she were to do this, the cruse of oil would never fail and the meal would never run out until the Lord sent rain upon the earth again.

And we have the results of her giving in these beautiful words, "And the barrel of meat wasted not, neither did the cruse of oil fail, according to the word of the Lord, which he spake by Elijah" (1 Kings 17:16).

When the disciples gave the bread and fish to the crowd first, our Lord made sure that there was ample left for their own needs. This is a biblical principle that we find from Genesis through Revelation. God looks after his own people—particularly if they look after others first.

Having said this, I believe it is important to mention the fact that the things God gives us on the basis of this principle may not be luxurious and affluent. In the story of the five-thousand the bread that was used was poor folks' fare. Only the poor made their bread out of barley. And we should note that they were dealing with dried fish, not a fatted calf. What was left over was only twelve baskets—not a hundred. It was only enough for the disciples.

What a source of encouragement it must have been to the church of Philippi when Paul wrote to them and assured them: "My God shall supply all your need according to his riches in glory by Christ Jesus" (Phil. 4:19).

Unfortunately, this promise has been badly abused. Abused, I think, because we have totally ignored the context in which Paul said this. In the first place he was in prison, and just before he made this statement he told the Philippians that he had learned in whatever condition he found himself to be content. You will remember that he said, "I know both how to be abased, and I know how to abound: every where and in all things I am instructed both to be full and to be hungry, both to abound and to suffer need" (Phil. 4:12). Paul quickly adds that he is not writing because he needs anything: "I have all, and abound: I am full, having received of Epaphroditus the things which were sent from you, an odour of a sweet smell, a sacrifice acceptable, well pleasing to God" (Phil. 4:18).

What Paul was thanking God for was probably an old coat, some books and some parchments, which he valued very highly. This is what he meant by "abounding." There is nothing luxurious about this, and again we should be reminded that this is the context in which he rejoices over the fact that, "My God shall supply all your needs."

In January of 1986 Billy Graham very graciously came to Toronto to preach at my father's funeral. It was interesting to be briefed on the arrangements that he would expect. Among other things he wanted to make sure that he was not met at the airport with a big luxurious car. It must not be a Cadillac, Mercedes Benz, Lincoln, or any other un-necessarily large or well-equipped vehicle. How I thank God for a man of Billy Graham's calibre, who does not think God owes him the luxuries of this world.

When I was a small boy, my brother, Glen, and I used to spend many of our summers on a farm about forty or fifty miles away from Toronto. It was back in the days when farms did not have electricity or running water. We got our water by pumps. There were several of the pumps that would not work unless first of all we poured a can of water into them. Any farmhand of course knows that this is called priming the pump. It will bring forth all the water you need, but you have to put some water into it first. This is one way of illustrating the principle of giving to God before we can expect to receive from God.

3. *There should be a balance in our lives between meeting people in the marketplace and meeting God in the secret place.*

It is true that much of our preaching zeroes in on activity. We are ex-pected to go to church. We should read our Bibles. It would be great if we were to teach a Sunday school class. We should sing in the choir, visit the sick and maybe even take an evening course at the local Bible college. This is important. The Bible is full of commands to be active. But our ac-tivity for God is only as valid as our fellowship with God. My father, Dr. Oswald J. Smith, was a songwriter. He wrote all kinds of songs, but it is interesting to note his own favorites. They were not "God Understands," "Then Jesus Came," "The Song of the Soul Set Free"

64

or any of the other rousing songs of service.

His favorite song was called "Alone With Thee." This was one of the few songs for which he wrote both the lyrics and the music. The poem was composed on August 30, 1914, at Winowna Lake, Indiana. The music was composed a year after in 1915 in Toronto. But he always considered this his own favorite among all of his songs. It went like this:

> Alone with thee, oh blessed, blissful moment!
> When earth recedes and thou art all my plea—
> I hear, dear Lord, amid the mystic stillness,
> Thy gentle voice while all alone with thee.
>
> Alone with thee, 'mid all earth's toil and labour—
> It matters not what ère my destiny;
> Tho' all around is bustle, strife, and worry,
> Yet still, dear Lord, I walk alone with thee.

I think that our time alone with God not only makes it possible for us to have a more powerful ministry, but I think there is ample biblical evidence to lead us to believe that our time alone with God will have an effect on our general appearance to other people—even though we do not say or do anything: "Now when they saw the boldness of Peter and John, and perceived that they were unlearned and ignorant men, they marvelled; and they took knowledge of them, that they had been with Jesus" (Acts 4:13). Obviously there was an expression on their faces that indicated that they had been in the presence of God. It was notable.

Moses had the same experience when he talked with God: "And it came to pass, when Moses came down from Mount Sinai with the two tables of testimony in Moses' hand, when he came down from the mount, that Moses wist not that the skin of his face shone while he talked with him" (Exod. 34:29). Moses was not even aware of what had happened, but the people were. There was something about his face that was different, and they noticed it immediately.

Part Three

From Tradition To The Word — Chapter 7
From Blindness To Sight — Chapter 8
From Earth To Heaven — Chapter 9

Then the Pharisees and scribes asked him, "Why walk not thy disciples according to the tradition of the elders, but eat bread with unwashen hands?" He answered and said unto them, "Well hath Esaias prophesied of you hypocrites, as it is written, 'This people honoureth me with their lips, but their heart is far from me. Howbeit in vain do they worship me, teaching for doctrines the commandments of men.' For laying aside the commandment of God, ye hold the tradition of men, as the washing of pots and cups: and many other such like things ye do." And he said unto them, "Full well ye reject the commandment of God, that ye may keep your own tradition."

Mark 7:5-9

Chapter 7

From Tradition to the Word

Our Lord's audiences usually consisted of the faithful disciples, the common people, and the religious critics. It is true that the disciples deserted Jesus when he was crucified, but we should always remember that when they followed him in the first place they gave up everything to do so. Those were the conditions of discipleship. We should also keep in mind that after the day of Pentecost these men were extremely faithful—faithful enough to follow their Lord through martyrdom. With the possible exception of the apostle John, every one of them died under the early persecutions of the Roman Empire. Of course, Judas died shortly after he had betrayed Jesus.

The common people formed by far the largest part of our Lord's crowds. They loved him because he was saying things that they had always wished to hear somebody in authority say. Most of these people wanted to do right and they were looking for answers. Jesus seemed to have the answers. The authority with which he spoke was a constant source of amazement to them.

Finally, there were the religious leaders, who made it a point to criticize everything he did. On this occasion they had come all the way from Jerusalem—a distance of more than fifty miles—to find fault. They did not want answers because the sort of answers Jesus was giving would force them to change their way of living.

"And when they saw some of his disciples eat bread with defiled, that is to say, with unwashen, hands, they found fault. Then the Pharisees and scribes asked him, Why walk not thy disciples according to the tradition of the elders, but eat bread with unwashen hands?" (Mark 7: 2,5).

Jesus responded to them by saying three things: 1) The word of God always takes precedence over the traditions of people; 2) The evil in the world does not make people bad. What makes them bad is the evil within themselves; 3) People are not righteous because of what they say or do. They are righteous because of what they are in their hearts.

The Word Versus Tradition

"How be it in vain do they worship me, teaching for doctrines the commandments of men. For laying aside the commandment of God, ye hold the tradition of men, as the washing of pots and cups: And many other such like things ye do. And he said unto them, "Full well ye reject the commandment of God, that ye may keep your own tradition" (Mark 7:7-8).

For the Jew, the Word of God in its most abbreviated form consisted of the ten commandments. In its most expanded form it would include all that was in the five books of Moses, to which the Jews had access in written form.

However, in addition to the written law there was an oral law that had come down through the generations. It had started four or five hundred years before Christ, introduced by the people who were called scribes. The scribes had taken the mosaic law and divided it into six hundred and thirteen separate decrees. They had further divided these decrees. There were three hundred and sixty-five of them that were negative. We might say they were the "don'ts" of the Jewish faith. The other two hundred and forty-eight of these decrees were positive. That is, they were the "do's" of the faith. In addition to all of these regulations there was an endless list of rules about each one of these decrees.

There were literally thousands of unclean things. After childbirth a woman was unclean. Anyone who touched a dead body was unclean.

70

Anyone who had touched a dead body made everything else that he touched unclean. A Gentile was unclean. Food that had been touched by a Gentile was unclean. A dishpan or utensil that had been touched by a Gentile was unclean. That is why a devout Jew had to take a complete ceremonial bath after he had been to market. That was the only way that he could become ceremonially clean once again. In our world we would probably use the word "taboo" in place of the word unclean.

These rules and regulations had not been reduced to writing during the days of Jesus. This was not done until two or three hundred years later in the Mishnah. To add to the burden of law that the Jews already carried, another written work, the Gemara, came into existence. The Gemara contained the comments of the rabbis from A.D. 200 to 500 on the regulations to be found in the Mishnah. The Mishnah and the Gemara formed part of the Jewish Talmud. The Talmud is the source from which Jewish law is derived. It is binding for faith and life on Orthodox Jews.

But the Talmud was not the Word of God. It was a collection of the oral traditions of the scribes, and sometimes they even found ways that they could get around the clearly written Word of God. This is what Jesus objected to. Everywhere he went he shouted: The written Word first! The opinions of people second! Never accept a tradition that violates the Word!

It would be a good exercise for us to check out our own modern Christian beliefs against the written Word of God. This is what Martin Luther, John Calvin and others were doing during the Protestant Reformation. They were testing the teachings of the Roman Catholic church against the written word of God. Is baptism necessary for salvation? Is observing the mass necessary for salvation? How does one pray to the Virgin Mary and the saints and at the same time accept the inescapable teaching of the written Word that there is only one Mediator between man and God. Where does the Bible teach that the pope or any other man or woman is infallible?

There were no valid answers to these questions in the days of the reformation, and they have still not been answered. That is why all of the leaders of the reformation refused to stay in the Roman Catholic church. When they discovered the truth, they left the church.

During all of my lifetime we have been sending missionaries to countries that have been dominated by the church of Rome. When people were converted in these countries they were never expected to stay in the Catholic church. How can one stay in a church that allows the traditions of man to take precedence over the written Word of God?

Evil Outside Versus Evil Inside

It would be easy for any of us to make a list of things that are evil, and it would be a very long list. Don't read dirty books. Don't visit the "red light" district. Don't look at *Playboy*, *Hustler* and other pornographic magazines. And the list goes on . . .

Our Lord's response to such a list was to say that what is bad is what is already in a man, leading him to respond to these things. It is something that is within us that reacts to these things: "There is nothing from without a man, that entering into him can defile him: but the things that come out of him, those are they that defile the man" (Mark 7:15).

We might abolish, do away with, ban or destroy all of these "evil things." However that would not change us. We would still be evil on the inside.

Actions Versus the Heart

These people were doing and saying all the right things. They were trying desperately to keep the multitude of regulations that had come down to them orally, but Jesus calls them *hypocrites*: "Well hath Esaias prophesied of you hypocrites, as it is written, This people honoureth me with their lips, but their heart is far from me" (Mark 7:6).

A hypocrite is one who acts a part. He is a person who pretends to be what he is not. He is a pretender. He pretends to be pious, virtuous, etc. without really being so.

This has been a problem in every generation. Jesus is quoting the prophet Isaiah here: "Wherefore the Lord said, This people draw near me with their mouth, and with their lips do honour me, but have removed their heart far from me, and their fear toward me is taught by the precept of man" (Isa. 29:13).

The world had not changed a great deal. What was a problem in the days of Isaiah was also a problem in the days of Jesus. The scribes and Pharisees were careful to observe all the rules. They went to the synagogue at the appropriate times. They wore the right clothes with the proper tassels. They read the right books. But Jesus saw through them and called them hypocrites.

Most Christian people are aware of the fact that the other religions of the world are built around doing and saying the right things. This is true of Hinduism, Mohammedanism, Judaism, Buddhism and Roman Catholicism. Sad to say, we often notice this kind of thing in others but fail to make the same test of our own faith. It is easy to do and say the things that evangelicals are supposed to. How do I prove that I am an evangelical? I go to a known evangelical church. I sing gospel songs and choruses. I go to a place where the services are conducted in a very informal manner. I know all of the proper language. I use such words as "the Bible," "saved," "blood," "born again," "testimony," etc. I am connected with the right people and organizations—Billy Graham, Youth for Christ, the Gideons, Faith Missions, Christian Business Men's committees, Inter-Varsity, Campus Crusade, Navigators, and the list goes on. I wonder if Jesus would say exactly the same thing to some of us as he said to the religious people of his day: "Your lips are saying the right things and your feet are taking you to the right places but your heart is far from me."

Jesus emphasized this principle, but it was not original with him. The entire Bible is full of it—both in the Old Testament and the New Testament: God is concerned about the purity of our hearts.

"For man looketh on the outward appearance, but the Lord looketh upon the heart." (1 Sam. 16:7).

"Create in me a clean heart, O God; and renew a right spirit in me" (Ps. 51:10).

"The Lord is nigh unto them that are of a broken heart" (Ps. 34:18).

"The heart is deceitful above all things, and desperately wicked: who can know it? I the Lord search the heart (Jer. 17:9-10).

"Daniel purposed in his heart that he would not defile himself with the portion of the king's meat, nor with the wine which he drank" (Dan. 1:8).

"But I say unto you, That whosoever looketh on a woman to lust after her hath committed adultery with her already in his heart" (Matt. 5:28).

"Turn ye even to me with all your heart, and with fasting, and with weeping, and with mourning: And rend your heart, and not your garments, and turn unto the Lord your God" (Joel 2:12-13).

"Search me, O God, and know my heart: try me, and know my

thoughts: And see if there be any wicked way in me, and lead me in the way everlasting'' (Ps. 139:23-24).

The principle is not that our actions are not unimportant to God but rather that our actions are motivated by what is in our hearts. Of course God knows what we are doing and may be concerned. God sees what we do, but people can see our actions too. But God sees something that man cannot see—our hearts. In most cases we need to deal with our heart problems. The actions will then follow automatically.

And he cometh to Bethsaida; and they bring a blind man unto him, and besought him to touch him. And he took the blind man by the hand, and led him out of the town; and when he had spit on his eyes, and put his hands upon him, he asked him if he saw ought. And he looked up, and said, "I see men as trees, walking." After that he put his hands again upon his eyes, and made him look up: and he was restored, and saw every man clearly. And he sent him away to his house, saying, "Neither go into the town, nor tell it to any in the town."

Mark 8:22-26

Chapter 8

From Blindness To Sight

The story of the healing of the blind man at Bethsaida is told only in the Gospel of Mark. Bethsaida had been Peter's home town (John 1:44). The apostle Peter remembered this story well and probably used it very often in his teaching. If the Gospel of Mark represents the teaching of the apostle Peter, then of course this story would be included in Mark's Gospel, even if it did not appear anywhere else. Or to put it another way, this would be one of the pieces of internal evidence that supports the idea that Mark did in fact record the teaching of Peter. This was the belief of the majority of the early church.

Bethsaida was also in all probability the area where Jesus fed the five thousand. It was located at the north end of the Sea of Galilee—not right on the coast, but inland about a half a mile.

Jesus performed this particular miracle in two stages. First of all, he put some of his own saliva on the man's blind eyes. This was not entirely without reason, since many people in those days believed that there was a certain amount of healing power in our saliva. As a matter of fact, we have not come very far from that in these past two thousand years. If we hit our finger with a hammer or stick a pin into it, most of us will instinctively put it in our mouths. After Jesus had anointed the man's eyes with his spittal, the man was able to see obscurely: "I see men as trees, walking."

There is a certain amount of similarity between the trunk of a tree and the trunk of a human body. As a matter of fact, we use exactly the same word to describe both. Almost everybody at some time or other has bumped into a tree or a lamp post at night, and apologized. We have mistaken it for a person. The point is that the man was able to see, but without clarity.

"After that he put his hands again upon his eyes, and made him look up: and he was restored, and saw every man clearly" (Mark 8:25).

I don't think this story is a good example of progressive, or gradual healing. This entire transaction may have taken a total of fifteen or twenty minutes—including the time it took Jesus to lead the blind man outside of the town before he performed the miracle. It would not compare for a moment with the multiple visits of sick people to modern faith healers—sometimes with the assurance that they were getting better gradually, just as this blind man was healed gradually. There is no comparison at all. However, what this story illustrates beautifully is partial and total healing of spiritual blindness.

In the Gospel of Mark the story of Peter's confession that Jesus Christ is the Messiah follows this healing incident immediately. Before Peter's confession the disciples had been told by Jesus that they were blind spiritually: "Having eyes, see ye not?" (Mark 8:18). After Peter's confession the disciples saw spiritually, but not clearly. Then after the cross and the resurrection, and before their own deaths, they saw clearly.

1. From total blindness to partial sight.

Peter's confession resulted from our Lord's question "Whom do men say that I am?" After the healing of the blind man Jesus and the disciples had walked about twenty-five miles north of the Sea of Galilee, and it was there at Caesarea Philippi that Peter's confession was made.

This was an area that was saturated with religious beliefs. It was thought to be the birthplace of the Greek god Pan—the god of nature and shepherds. There was a marble temple there that had been erected to Augustus Caesar by Herod the Great, and later it was further adorned by his son Herod Philip, the Tetrarch. This was one of the many temples to the emperor throughout the ancient world in which people were forced to proclaim that "Caesar is Lord!" When the early Christians refused to do this, they were accused of treason. They were in an area in which it was hard to get away from the idea that the emperor of the Romans was god.

Caesarea Philippi was also very near to the source of the Jordan River. It was here that Baal had been worshipped in Old Testament days, and, of course, it was an area pregnant with Jewish history. Jesus had taken the disciples to a place where they were surrounded by religions of one kind or another—including the Jewish faith. It was in this setting that our Lord asked, "Whom do men say that I am?"

In other words, what is the opinion of the general public. What rumors have you been hearing? The disciples gave three answers. The first was—"Some people are saying that you are John the Baptist." And of course there were some similarities between Jesus and John. They were almost the same age. Only six months separated them. They were both preachers and teachers. To some extent they were both proclaiming some ideas that seemed to be revolutionary. When Herod Antipas heard about Jesus and all of the miracles he was performing, he thought that John the Baptist, the man whom he had beheaded, had been resurrected (Mark 6:16).

The second answer was—"There are others that think you are Elijah." Of course, the people knew that Elijah had never died and that the final prophesy of the Old Testament was to the effect that some day Elijah would return: "Behold, I will send you Elijah the prophet before the coming of the great and dreadful day of the Lord" (Mal. 4:5).

Their third reply was—"Still others believe that you are one of the other prophets." Matthew adds a third name to this list—the prophet Jeremiah (Matt. 16:14).

All of these were good answers and all were saying a very honorable thing about Jesus. They were actually saying that he could be compared to any one of the Old Testament prophets. By no means derogatory remarks, these answers proved the tremendous respect that the people had for him. They all recognized the fact that he was an extremely unusual person. In conversation they probably would have said that he would go down in history.

These were good answers, excellent answers. But they were not good enough. There was indeed a certain amount of truth in what the people were saying. Our Lord could be compared favorably with almost any of the Old Testament prophets. As a matter of fact, he might even be considered a composite model of all of the Old Testament prophets. That would make him a superprophet. The best. They were making statements that were partial truths about Jesus.

This is one of the great dangers of the other religions of the world and many philosophical viewpoints. This is the danger of the false cults who claim to be Christian: all of them contain partial truths in their beliefs, otherwise they could never even get off the ground as religions or good philosophies for anybody. The humanistic materialist would not deny that Jesus was a great man. In fact, I have often heard people say that Jesus was one of their personal heroes. This would be the position of the agnostic, for most agnostics would not make belittling remarks about Jesus.

These would be the answers of the false cults. All of the false cults claim to be Christian and they believe a great deal of the Bible—maybe even most of the Bible. When they knock on our doors, almost everything they say sounds familiar to us because it is similar to what we have been taught in Sunday school all of our lives. But they are dangerous because they represent partial truth.

These would be the answers of liberal theologians and ministers. Liberal seminaries could not even call themselves Christian if they did not believe a great deal of the truth about Jesus Christ. They might even accept eighty-five or ninety percent of what the Bible says about Jesus, but once again they teach a partial truth. And that is the kind of truth that is the most dangerous. It is the most damaging weapon of the devil.

All of these may believe in Jesus. They may believe most of what the Bible says about Jesus, but they fall just short of admitting that he is God. Herein lies their spiritual blindness. They are not bad people, satanic people, mean people, dirty people or unkind people. They may be the nicest folk in the world, the most loving, the kindest, the most philanthropic, the most generous, the most helpful. However, they are dangerous because they fall short of accepting the deity of our Lord. They are spiritually blind—just as the blind man of Bethsaida. They were like the disciples before Peter's confession—"Having eyes, see ye not?"

Any view of Jesus that makes him less than God represents spiritual blindness. It is interesting to notice that Mark puts this particular story at the heart of his Gospel. But not only is the deity of Christ at the heart of the Gospel positionally—it is located in approximately the centre of the chapters—but it is the heart of the Gospel in the sense that there is no gospel without the deity of Christ. Just as there is no life in a body without the heart.

After the disciples had answered Jesus' first question, he asked them the crucial question: "But whom say ye that I am?" Now our Lord was asking the disciples to get out of the grandstand and come down on the playing field. Don't be satisfied to let other people carry the ball. It is time for you to run with the ball yourselves, even though you may be running in the opposite direction of popular opinion.

Peter responded immediately, "Thou art the Christ." Luke gives our Lord's answer a little differently, "the Christ of God." Matthew is also slightly different, "Thou art the Christ, the Son of the living God."

Peter was no longer totally blind as he had been before the healing of the blind man. However, after the confession our Lord was very quick to tell the disciples that they should not pass this information on to anybody: "He charged them that they should tell no man of him." I think the reason for this was that although they now had some spiritual sight, like the blind man of Bethsaida, they were not able to see clearly. They had partial sight. They had obscured sight. They were able to see, but indistinctly.

2. From partial sight to 20/20 vision.

The disciples had seen that Jesus was the Messiah. He was indeed God. But what they had not seen clearly was the fact that the Messiah would have to suffer and die. The prophets of the Old Testament had predicted that one like King David would come to take over the throne of his father. It would be a real throne in this world that would introduce a time of unprecedented peace and prosperity. However, before this kingdom came about, there would be a period of great tribulation, and toward the end of this tribulation Elijah would return as the forerunner of the Messiah. The Messiah would come as a world conqueror to defeat all of the enemies of the Jews. He would establish a kingdom that would centre in Palestine and from there rule the entire world. It was generally believed that the Old Testament prophesied that this kingdom would then last for ever.

Of course the disciples would have shared this prophetic picture with the rest of their people. When they left everything to follow Jesus, they expected that he would establish a kingdom; but they thought of that kingdom as here and now, very physical and material, and they thought of themselves as the ministers of state. That is why Jesus insisted that they say nothing about the fact that he was the Messiah—the confession that Peter had made, probably for himself and for all of the other disciples as well. Peter was generally their spokesman.

Jesus insisted that they say nothing because, although they saw now that he was the Messiah, their vision of his kingdom was very blurred, indistinct and obscure. They were like the blind man after Jesus put the

79

spittle on his eyes. He saw men as trees walking. He was no longer totally blind, but his sight was still partially impaired.

What the disciples did not realize about the kingdom was that the King had to die before he reigned, and furthermore, his followers would have to suffer a great many things before the kingdom was established: "And he began to teach them, that the Son of man must suffer many things, and be rejected of the elders, and of the chief priests, and scribes, and be killed, and after three days rise again" (Mark 8:31).

This was unthinkable to partially blind Peter. The Messiah must not suffer. The Messiah must not die. For the Messiah there must be no cross. That's why once again Peter spoke for the rest of the disciples and objected, whereupon Jesus "rebuked Peter, saying, Get thee behind me, Satan: for thou savourest not the things that be of God, but the things that be of men" (Mark 8:33).

At the centre of the Christian faith is the deity of Christ: "Thou art the Christ." At the centre of the Christian faith is the cross: "The Son of man must be killed." At the centre of the Christian faith is the broken body of Christ and the shed blood of Christ: "The Son of man must suffer many things."

But there was more. Not only would the Messiah have to suffer and die, but Jesus also told them that if they followed him and believed in him they would also have to suffer for his sake. The disciples simply refused to believe this. Then Jesus called the crowd over to where they were having this discussion. Apparently they had withdrawn a little distance from the crowd and Peter had made his confession only to Jesus and his fellow disciples, but then our Lord turned His attention back to the crowd and explained what he had been talking about: "Whosoever will come after me, let him deny himself, and take up his cross, and follow me" (Mark 8:34).

This was devastating to the disciples. They were interested in power and position. They were interested in such things as "Who is the greatest in the kingdom of heaven?" (Matt. 18:1). James and John actually asked Jesus for special positions: "Grant unto us that we may sit, one on thy right hand, and the other on thy left hand, in thy glory" (Mark 10:37).

In Matthew's Gospel he tells this story, leaving the impression that James and John had actually got their mother to ask Jesus for these positions on behalf of her sons: "Grant that these my two sons may sit, the one on thy right hand, and the other on the left, in thy kingdom" (Matt. 20:21).

It was this desire for position that brought about our Lord's demonstration of foot washing in the upper room. This was to show the disciples that following him was not a life of commanding but of serving. Jesus went directly from the upper room and this demonstration of serving the disciples to Gethsemane and the cross. Christian service involves suffering. It involved suffering and death for the Master. It may involve death for those who follow him. Certainly, it will involve suffering of some kind.

Modern Christians are still very much like the disciples. Very logically they say: "Surely God wants his people to be happy? Surely God wants his people to be physically well? Surely God wants his people to prosper? Surely God wants his people to live like the children of the King?"

Our Lord would answer yes to all of these questions, but I think he would put it in the terminology of a great Scottish preacher of the last generation, James McGinley—"Not now, but afterwards." When I was a sophomore in Bob Jones University, Dr. McGinley came to the Bible conference that was held once a year. The only sermon that I remember was one he entitled "Not Now, but Afterwards." You see, McGinley's vision had been clarified. He was able to see things as they were—not "men as trees walking." He recognized the fact that the Christian faith was associated with unbelievable blessing and riches and honor and power and delights that were unimaginable. But he also realized that most of these would not happen now in this life, but afterwards in the next life.

That is what Jesus was attempting to get across to his disciples, and that is what they had the most difficulty understanding. It was not until after the cross and after the resurrection that it began to sink into their befuddled human minds—that Christianity involved suffering for the Savior and suffering for the people who followed him.

Certainly it is true that there are some prosperous Christians. However, they are few and far between—both in the world today and throughout the history of the church. The majority of God's people have suffered hardships of every kind and have even spent a great part of their lives in some form of captivity.

Our Christian people in North America and in a few of the other Christian countries of the world have enjoyed prosperity, but even in North America we can count the extremely prosperous Christians in a very short time. There are not many of them.

Furthermore, the poverty and captivity of Christians around the world is usually a result of the fact that they are Christians. It is not simply that they happen to live in a country where the people are behind barbed wire. It is because they have chosen to stand for Jesus Christ.

The true believer is a person who is willing to go upstream, regardless of how difficult it may be. He is a man who is not afraid to fly in the face of popular opinion. He is one who dares to be different. He is ready to reject the inadequate opinions of men in favor of the truth of God. He is a person who has moved from a concern for self to a reckless abandon to the will of God. The kingdom of God is for vigorous people.

Joseph could have had all of the luxuries of Egypt together with his master's wife. But Joseph was a man of God, and he refused the advances of Potiphar's wife: "But he refused, and said unto his master's wife, Behold, my master wotteth not what is with me in the house, and he hath committed all that he hath to my hand; . . . how then can I do this great wickedness, and sin against God?" (Gen. 39:8-9).

When Moses sent the spies into the Promised Land, they brought back this report: These people are strong. Their cities are walled and are very great. If we were to go into that land, the land would eat us up. The men are huge—like giants. Compared to them we are like grasshoppers. When they brought back this report the people were afraid and said, "Would God that we had died in the land of Egypt! or would God that we had died in this wilderness!" (Num. 14:2).

However, two of them were men of God, and they were not afraid to stand in opposition to the majority. Caleb and Joshua spoke to all of the people when they heard their complaint and said: "The land, which we passed through to search it, is an exceeding good land. If the Lord delight in us, then he will bring us into this land, and give it us; a land which floweth with milk and honey. Only rebel not ye against the Lord, neither fear ye the people of the land; for they are bread for us: their defence is departed from them, and the Lord is with us: fear them not" (Num. 14:7-9).

When the great king Nebuchadnezzar ordered the people to bow down and worship the golden image, most of them did it. They had a very good reason to obey this command because the king had said that if anyone did not bow down and worship the image, he would be thrown into a red-hot fiery furnace.

However, once again there were three men of God—Shadrach, Meshach and Abednego. When the bugles blew, they did not bow down. When they were brought before the king, they gave him a remarkable answer: "If it be so, our God whom we serve is able to deliver us from the burning fiery furnace, and he will deliver us out of thine hand O king. But if not, be it known unto thee, O king, that we will not serve thy gods, nor worship the golden image which thou hast set up" (Dan. 3:17-18).

In other words, we will be faithful to our God. If he saves us from the fire, that is great! If he does not save us from the fire, it does not matter! We are going to obey his orders rather than yours, no matter what it costs. Shadrach, Meshach and Abednego were God's people, and God's people dare to be different—even if it hurts.

The apostles Peter and John healed a lame man who was stationed every day at one of the gates of the temple—the gate Beautiful. When they were picked up and questioned by the religious leaders, they preached to them about the resurrection of Jesus Christ. They were told that they must never preach about him again. But Peter and John stood right up to them and said, "Whether it be right in the sight of God to hearken unto you more than unto God, judge ye. For we cannot but speak the things which we have seen and heard" (Acts 4:19-20).

Peter and John were followers of Jesus and were not afraid to take a position in opposition to the crowd. What a difference from their attitude before the cross! Then they wanted position, power and prosperity. Now they wanted only to serve Jesus Christ and bring the gospel to the world, regardless of the price they had to pay personally.

Stephen, the first martyr, was stoned for the same kind of reckless abandonment that had now become the characteristic of all the early Christians. When he preached, he accused them of many things. He actually called them a "stiff-necked people" and said, "You are fighting against the Holy Ghost. Your fathers persecuted the prophets, and you have not even kept the laws of Moses." Stephen had reached the place of abandonment. He had stopped thinking only of himself and he had given himself completely to the will of God, regardless of what the cost might be.

In his last days in a Roman prison, as we have already seen, the apostle Paul said that he knew how to abound and how to be abased. If it was necessary to suffer, he was willing to do so. "I know both how to be abased, and I know how to abound: every where and in all things I am instructed both to be full and to be hungry, both to abound and to suffer need. I can do all things through Christ which strengtheneth me" (Phil. 4:12-13).

The apostle Paul never looked for perfect health or great prosperity or high position. He sought only to serve Jesus Christ—either to witness to his saving grace or to suffer for him.

When the disciples finally learned the principle of the suffering servant, for the first time they were able to see distinctly. Their eyes had been opened. They were no longer blind. Partial sight came when they realized that Jesus was the Messiah. Still more clearly were they able to see when they knew and accepted the fact that Jesus had to die. Their complete vision was not reached until they understood that they would have to suffer and that they might also have to die if they followed Jesus.

There is a final clarity of sight that will be realized after this life: "For now we see through a glass, darkly; but then face to face: now I know in part; but then shall I know even as also I am known" (1 Cor. 13:12).

And after six days Jesus taketh with him Peter, and James, and John, and leadeth them up into an high mountain apart by themselves: and he was transfigured before them. And his raiment became shining, exceeding white as snow; so as no fuller on earth can white them. And there appeared unto them Elias with Moses: and they were talking with Jesus. And Peter answered and said to Jesus, "Master, it is good for us to be here: and let us make three tabernacles; one for thee, and one for Moses, and one for Elias." For he wist not what to say; for they were sore afraid. And there was a cloud that overshadowed them: and a voice came out of the cloud, saying, "This is my beloved Son: hear him." And suddenly, when they had looked round about, they saw no man any more, save Jesus only with themselves.

Mark 9:2-8

Chapter 9

From Earth to Heaven

Christ our Savior, in the Gospel of St. Matthew, hearing the confession of Simon Peter, who, first of all other, openly acknowledged him to be the Son of God, and perceiving the secret hand of His Father therein, called him (alluding to his name) a rock upon which rock he would build His Church so strong that the gates of hell should not prevail against it. In which words three things are to be noted: First, that Christ will have a Church in this world. Secondly, that the same Church should mightily be impugned, not only by the world, but also by the uttermost strength and powers of all hell. And, thirdly, that the same Church, notwithstanding the uttermost of the devil and all his malice, should continue.

This is the first paragraph in *Foxe's Book of Martyrs*.

Jesus attempted throughout his ministry on many occasions to explain to the disciples the hard facts of the gospel—not only that he would suffer and die, but that if they were to follow him, they could expect the same kind of trouble. These prophetic utterances of our Lord have been repeated again and again throughout the world in every century. John Foxe's *Book of Martyrs* tells the story of the suffering of Christians during the first century and during his own lifetime—that infamous time that we refer to as the Inquisition. However, similar stories can be found in almost every century of the Christian church. The people who follow Jesus may expect suffering at the hands of the world.

However, Jesus did not leave us with a hopeless picture. He declared that the kingdom of God would in fact come in power, and furthermore, he said that some of the people to whom he talked would see that day: "Verily I say unto you, That there be some of them that stand here, which shall not taste of death, till they have seen the kingdom of God come with power" (Mark 9:1).

Some of these people did in fact live long enough to see strong evidence that the kingdom of God had come in power. The first of these evidences of course would be the resurrection. The angel at the empty tomb declared it to the women who had come to anoint his body, "He is not here: for he is risen, as he said" (Matt. 28:6).

They saw further evidence of the kingdom coming in power when the Holy Spirit came on the Day of Pentecost. On that day the disciples must have remembered his promise that this would happen: "I will not leave you comfortless: I will come to you. But the Comforter, which is the Holy Ghost, whom the Father will send in my name, he shall teach you all things" (John 14:18,26).

They also saw the explosion of the church during the first century. During his lifetime Jesus had only been outside of Palestine on three occasions—once when he was taken as a baby to Egypt, once when he had gone with the disciples to the area of Tyre and Sidon, and once when he went through Samaria. Our Lord's personal ministry was to a very small group of people, in a country that was insignificant in world affairs. Palestine is only one hundred and twenty miles from north to south and forty miles from east to west. During our Lord's life there may have been only four million people there. And the Jewish leaders of the day had him killed, on the trumped-up charge that he was a threat to Caesar. Certainly, the future of Christianity looked totally hopeless.

But within the lifetime of many of the people who heard him, the Christian faith had swept throughout Asia Minor, it had penetrated Egypt, it had reached Rome and had been well established in Greece. Indeed, the kingdom of God had come in power.

A few of the people to whom our Lord ministered lived long enough to see the fall of Jerusalem. By this time most of the disciples, if not all of them, had died, but there were still people living who would have remembered his predictions about this event. "And when ye shall see Jerusalem encompassed with armies, then know that the desolation thereof is nigh. And Jerusalem shall be trodden down of the Gentiles, until the times of the Gentiles be fulfilled" (Luke 21:20,24).

This took place under the leadership of Titus in A.D. 70, just nine years before he became the Roman emperor. This might have been thought of as the return of Christ in judgment—another evidence that the kingdom had come in power.

However, what Jesus meant by the coming of the kingdom of God in power was much more than all of these victories combined. In the first ten verses of the ninth chapter of Mark's gospel we find the story of the transfiguration. Jesus allowed three of the disciples to see the total picture of his power.

He took Peter and James and John up Mount Hermon. Mount Hermon was located about seventeen or eighteen miles northeast of Caesarea Philippi. It was over nine thousand feet high—the most conspicuous mountain in Palestine. In all probability Jesus and his three disciples went only part of the way up Mount Hermon. But from here they would have been able to see traces of snow on the two upper peaks, even in the summer.

Why Jesus chose these three among the twelve we can only speculate upon. On the other hand, we might ask the question, why did Jesus choose the twelve among all of the other fine young Jewish men in Palestine? Certainly the answer has nothing to do with favoritism; but perhaps it has to do with the sovereignty of God. It may be that Jesus realized that these three understood what he was trying to tell them better than the others. This was one of three occasions on which Peter and James and John had been with Jesus apart from the others. One time was when he healed the daughter of Jairus and the other was when he went into the Garden of Gethsemane to pray.

Peter was obviously the spokesman for the rest of the disciples, and he was the first to express out loud that Jesus was the Christ. Many years later Peter referred to the transfiguration to vindicate his authority,

For we have not followed cunningly devised fables, when we made known unto you the power and coming of our Lord Jesus Christ, but were eye-witnesses of his majesty. For he received from God the Father honor and glory, when there came such a voice to him from the excellent glory, "This is my beloved Son, in whom I am well pleased." And this voice which came from heaven we heard, when we were with him in the holy mountain (2 Pet. 1:16-18).

James was destined to be one of the very early martyrs. He was beheaded by Herod Agrippa, probably in A.D. 44 (Acts 12:1-2). Peter's crucifixion was much later—probably during the persecutions of Nero in about A.D. 67.

Maybe John was there because he was destined to live the longest. He would write five of the books of the Bible, including the book of Revelation, which was written totally about the coming in power of the kingdom. John is probably referring to the transfiguration when he says in his first chapter, "And we beheld his glory, the glory as of the only begotten of the Father" (John 1:14).

Of all the Old Testament prophets Jesus chose Moses and Elijah to make an appearance on the Mount of Transfiguration. Moses was the great law-giver. Moses gave the law and Christ fulfilled the law. The apostle Philip had a very early intuition of this. When he went to bring his friend Nathanael to Jesus, he told him, "We have found him, of whom Moses in the law, and the prophets, did write, Jesus of Nazareth, the son of Joseph" (John 1:45).

A great deal of what Jesus said in the Sermon on the Mount was to show that he had come to fulfil the law of Moses, "Think not that I am come to destroy the law, or the prophets: I am not come to destroy, but to fulfill" (Matt. 5:17). Moses had been buried by God. He would represent all of those both in the Old Testament and the New Testament who were God's people, but had died and had been buried.

Elijah may have been the greatest prophet. It was Elijah who had prophesied in some detail the death of the Lord Jesus Christ—probably without realizing himself the significance of what he was saying or even that he was talking about the Messiah. Elijah did not die but was translated. He would therefore represent all of those who are alive when the Lord returns.

Moses and Elijah had prophesied about Jesus and had prefigured him. Now they gave place to him on the Mount of Transfiguration. On the Mount of Transfiguration, therefore, we have representatives of the redeemed people of God of all ages. The prophets represented all of the Old Testament saints and the apostles all of the New Testament saints. These five men represented all of those who have gone to be with the Lord. They represented those from my church and your church, from my family and your family. These are the people to whom the writer of the book of Hebrews was referring when he said, "Wherefore seeing we also are compassed about with so great a cloud of witnesses, let us lay aside every weight, and the sin which doth so easily beset us, and let us run with patience the race that is set before us" (Heb. 12:1).

It was in this holy place that Peter and James and John heard the voice of God which came out of the cloud saying, "This is my beloved Son: Hear him."

God was confirming what Jesus had been telling them. The cross is a fact. The resurrection is a fact. The suffering of his followers is a fact, and the Second Coming will also be a fact.

It is interesting also to notice the subject of their conversation on this august occasion. They did not talk about politics. They might have discussed the fall of Jerusalem or the breakup of the Roman empire or the problems of Palestine under Roman rule.

They might have discussed some of the theological problems of the day. Should they follow the teachings of Hillel or Shammai? Both had been prominent rabbis. They did not discuss eternal security or the possibility of falling from grace. They did not even discuss the important ministry of the Holy Spirit.

They did not discuss morality. There was no talk about abortion or divorce or remarriage or minority rights or even slavery.

There was no discussion of entertainment. Whether the "Jerusalem Blue Jays" would beat the "Damascus White Sox" in the game next weekend apparently was not important. They did not discuss music—either traditional and conservative or modern and liberal. There was no discussion of the evils of alcohol or drugs or even overeating.

Finally, there was no discussion of world catastrophes—either in the world at that time or those that would take place in the centuries that lay ahead. World Wars I, II or III were not mentioned. The ghastly starvation in Africa that stretches from the Atlantic to the Red Sea was given no time whatever in that conversation.

It is Luke that fills in the subject of their discussion. "And, behold, there talked with him two men, which were Moses and Elias: Who appeared in glory, and spake of his decease which he should accomplish at Jerusalem" (Luke 9:30,31). The only topic was the cross and the death of our Lord. You see, it is the cross that is the door to heaven. It is the cross that makes possible our adoption into the family of God. It is the cross that is our ransom for sin, the offering for our souls and the substitution for our death.

It seems strange, said one of the ancient Christian writers, that in his exaltation they spoke of his suffering. That on Mount Hermon they should talk of Mount Calvary. That when his head shone with glory they should talk about the time it must bleed with thorns. That when his face glistened like the sun they should talk about the fact that it would be scratched, spit upon and rendered unrecognizable. That when his garments glittered they should talk about the fact that they would be stripped from him and divided among soldiers in a dice game. That when he was adored by the saints of heaven they should talk about the fact that he would be scorned by the basest of men. That when he was seen between two patriarchs they would talk about the fact that he would hang between two thieves. That when he was transfigured on the holy mountain they would talk about how he would be disfigured on the ugly cross.

The cross is never out of place. This subject is the most important to all of us. It is the most glorifying to God. That is why it is the most frequent topic to be discussed in our hymns here on earth:

> In the cross of Christ I glory,
> Towering o'er the wrecks of time:
> All the light of sacred story
> Gathers round its head sublime.
>
> John Bowring

> Mercy there was great, and grace was free;
> Pardon there was multiplied to me;
> There my burdened heart found liberty—
> At Calvary.
>
> William R. Newell

> I must needs go home by the way of the cross,
> There is no other way but this;
> I shall ne'er get sight of the gates of light,
> If the way of the cross I miss.
>
> Jessie Brown Pounds

> Have you been to Jesus for the cleansing power?
> Are you washed in the blood of the lamb?
> Are you fully trusting in his grace this hour?
> Are you washed in the blood of the lamb?
>
> Elisha J. Hoffman

Sing, oh, sing of my Redeemer,
With his blood he purchased me,
On the cross he sealed my pardon,
Paid the debt, and made me free.

Philip P. Bliss

———

Jesus paid it all,
All to him I owe;
Sin had left a crimson stain,
He washed it white as snow.

Elvina M. Hall

———

Beneath the cross of Jesus I feign would take my stand,
The shadow of a mighty rock within a weary land;
A home within the wilderness, a rest upon the way,
From the burning of the noontide heat,
And the burden of the day.

I take, oh cross, thy shadow, for my abiding place:
I ask no other sunshine, than the sunshine of his face;
Content to let the world go by, to know no gain nor loss,
My sinful self, my only shame,
My glory all the cross.

Elizabeth C. Clephane

Not only is it one of the major themes of our hymns here on earth, but it will also be the major theme of the praises to God in heaven: "And they sang a new song, saying, Thou art worthy to take the book, and to open the seals thereof: for thou wast slain, and hast redeemed us to God by thy blood out of every kindred, and tongue, and people, and nation" (Rev. 5:9).

When we meet one another in this world we salute with such phrases as Hello! Good Day! How are you! Perhaps in heaven our salute to one another when we meet will be such phrases as The Cross! Worthy is the Lamb! Jesus died for us!

As we have already seen, the people on the Mount of Transfiguration represented all of the redeemed of all ages. Moses, Elijah, Peter, James and John are typical of the Old Testament saints and the New

Testament saints—the Old Testament church and the New Testament church. It is quite obvious that when they met they knew each other. The disciples did not need anybody to tell them who Moses and Elijah were. It seems that they already knew that. The disciples knew the prophets and it is safe to assume that the prophets knew the disciples.

Sometimes we ask the question, "Will we know each other in heaven?" I believe the answer to that question is an emphatic yes! Not only will we know all of the people we have ever met in this world, but we will also know those people whom we never met—those who lived centuries before our time and those who may live many years after our time. There will be no strangers in heaven.

The pastor will know his people. Prayer warriors will know those who have been on their prayer lists. Missionaries will know their prayer backers. Sunday school teachers will know their students. Personal workers will know those whom they led to Christ. The evangelists will know their converts.

On the Mount of Transfiguration the disciples were there, the prophets were there, and God was there. Moses heard from God on Mount Sinai (Exod. 19:3). Elijah heard from God on a mountain (1 Kings 19:11). Now centuries later, Moses and Elijah once again hear from God on a mountain—Mount Hermon.

The voice of God came out of a cloud. Before God gave the children of Israel manna, he spoke to Moses out of a cloud (Exod. 16:10-12). Again, when God gave Moses the law, he spoke to him out of a cloud (Exod. 19:16-25). Again, when God spoke to Moses in the tabernacle for the first time, he spoke out of a cloud (Exod. 33:8-9). The first time the priest made sacrifices in Solomon's temple, a cloud filled the house of the Lord (1 Kings 8:10-11). The Jews firmly believed that when the Messiah came, that cloud would return to the temple. In their minds the voice of God was associated with a cloud. On the Mount of Transfiguration God spoke from a cloud.

Finally, Jesus was there on the mount. Mark tells us that he was "transfigured."

His clothes were shining—as white as snow. They were whiter than any "fuller" on earth could make them. A fuller is a person who does laundry. In Matthew's account he tells us that his face shone like the sun, and that his clothes were as white as light. In Luke's account he says that the fashion of his countenance was altered.

On the Mount of Transfiguration the disciples saw their Master in his pre-existent heavenly form—perfect, radiant, and eternal. Surely this experience must have been in the mind of the apostle John when he wrote,

Behold, what manner of love the Father hath bestowed upon us, that we should be called the sons of God: therefore the world knoweth us not, because it knew him not. Beloved, now are we the sons of God, and it doth not yet appear what we shall be: but we know that, when he shall appear, we shall be like him; for we shall see him as he is (1 John 3:1-2).

What a prospect!

It would be wonderful if I, or anybody else, could pray for you and guarantee that God would heal you physically. However, I have been in the ministry for more than forty-eight years and I can count on the fingers of both hands, or less, the people that I have known that have been dramatically healed. Without exception, everybody gets sick and dies—including those who claim to have the gift of healing. That is what this is all about. We suffer because of the original curse. We may suffer even more because we are Christians. The idea that Christians can claim healing is theological hogwash and scriptural balderdash.

Apart from those who may be living when the Lord Jesus Christ returns, all of us will eventually get sick and die. Whether that sickness comes suddenly, or whether it is slow, inevitably it will come. Thank God for an occasional person whom he dramatically heals. But these are the exceptions, not the rule. Many times I have prayed for people and anointed them with oil together with the elders of our church. However, I am very careful that I do not demand healing for these people. If I did, I would be doomed to disappointment, because in the majority of cases it does not happen.

What we can claim without fear of disappointment whatsoever is that someday we will be complete in Christ—both physically and in every other way. However, that is not a claim that we can make now. It is a claim to which we can look forward afterwards—after this life is over.

It was the German philosopher Bruno Bauer who said that religion is the "opium of the people." When he said this, he was referring to what I have just explained—that the final solution of all our problems is not in this world but in the next. However, this "opium" is something that the unbeliever does not have. At best, those who do not know Jesus Christ as their Savior have no painkiller that helps them through the difficulties that we face in this world. At worst, the unbeliever dies and goes to hell.

No wonder our hymns are filled with this theme, just as they are filled with the theme of the cross:

Home sweet home, home sweet home
Where I'll never roam.
I see the light of that city so bright,
My home, sweet home.

N.B. Vandall

Part Four

A Goodness That Doesn't Save—Chapter 10
A Shortcut That Leads to Nowhere—Chapter 11
A Recklessness That Pleases God—Chapter 12

And when he was gone forth into the way, there came one running, and kneeled to him, and asked him, "Good Master, what shall I do that I may inherit eternal life?" And Jesus said unto him, "Why callest thou me good? there is none good but one, that is, God. Thou knowest the commandments, Do not commit adultery, Do not kill, Do not steal, Do not bear false witness, Defraud not, Honor thy father and mother." And he answered and said unto him, "Master, all these have I observed from my youth." Then Jesus beholding him loved him, and said unto him, "One thing thou lackest: go thy way, sell whatsoever thou hast, and give to the poor, and thou shalt have treasure in heaven: and come, take up the cross, and follow me." And he was sad at that saying, and went away grieved: for he had great possessions.

Mark 10:17-22

Chapter 10

A Goodness That Doesn't Save

Perhaps our Lord's confrontation with the rich young ruler is the best-remembered section of chapter ten. However, there are many other important things in this chapter, including his discourse about divorce, his love for little children, more predictions regarding his death, the struggle for position among his disciples—who should sit on his right hand and left hand—and finally, the healing of Bartimaeus, the blind man.

The story of the rich young ruler occurs in approximately the middle of the chapter. This young man was obviously eager to get some answers to his questions—he came running. He also demonstrated a great deal of reverence for Jesus. He kneeled, then spoke to Jesus as one would speak to one's superior. He called him Good Master. There was nothing about his approach that expressed mere idle curiosity, nor was he making any attempt to trick Jesus, as the religious leaders had been trying to do from the beginning. He asked an extremely serious question, "Good Master, what shall I do that I may inherit eternal life?'' (Mark 10:17).

However, he made the mistake that many have made—that is, he thought there was something he could do in order to earn his salvation. He had failed to realize that salvation was not his to gain by his own efforts, but rather God's to give through his grace: "For by grace are ye saved through faith; and that not of yourselves: it is the gift of God: Not of works, lest any man should boast" (Eph. 2:8-9).

In addition to this, he very sincerely thought that he was a good man. He really believed that he had kept all of the commandments of Moses, "Master, all these have I observed from my youth" (Mark 10:20). However, in his heart he realized that there was something missing. Otherwise he would not have come to Jesus in the first place. Our Lord's answer must have been a great shock to this young man as well as to the others who were standing around listening to the conversation, "One thing thou lackest: go thy way, sell whatsoever thou hast, and give to the poor, and thou shalt have treasure in heaven: and come, take up the cross, and follow me" (Mark 10:21).

We should be very careful to notice that Jesus was not telling him that the way to have everlasting life was to give away his possessions. As far as we know, this is the only time Jesus ever told anybody to do this. What our Lord was concerned about was the fact that in this young man's case his wealth had become an obstacle that was keeping him from God. He was leaning on his material possessions. They had been a sort of a prop to him—a crutch.

In some cases wealth is not a support system that keeps people from God, but in the rich young ruler's case it was. This man was not an isolated example of this. There are many people who rely upon their material resources and therefore do not have an awareness of their need for God. Usually it is easier for a poor man to admit his need than it is for a rich man to do so. The trouble with material possessions is that they give us a false sense of security.

Although most of us will never be wealthy in material possessions, all of us have something that we lean upon and that we must totally abandon if we are going to accept Jesus Christ as our Savior. With some of us it is intellectual pride. With some it is our position in life. With some it is our family relationships. With some it is our friends. With some it is somebody we love. In every case Jesus would give to us exactly the same answer as he gave this man. Go, and get rid of your intellectual pride. Go, and renounce your position. Go, and separate yourself from your family. Go, and leave your old friends behind. Go, and give up your lover. I think most of us know exactly what area in our lives is separating us from God. Our Lord demands a total abandonment to him—no matter how great the sacrifice may be. With this man it happened to be his wealth, and he seemed unwilling to relinquish it, even for everlasting life.

In chapter four of this Gospel Jesus lists a number of other things that can also keep us from God: "The cares of this world, and the deceitfulness of riches, and the lusts of other things entering in, choke the word, and it becometh unfruitful" (Mark 4:19).

However, forsaking something or somebody who is dear to us in this life and totally abandoning them will not guarantee everlasting life. There are thousands of people who have given up a great deal for their heathen gods, but of course do not have eternal life. It is certainly true that these kinds of things must be forsaken, but that is only half of it. It is also necessary that we accept Jesus Christ as our Savior.

When this young man turned and went away, even though he was sad, he proved that he was more interested in his possessions than he was in eternal life. He had allowed his material wealth to keep him from becoming a child of God.

In our Lord's day the Jews had a tendency to associate wealth with righteousness. They thought that if a man prospered it was because he was a good man. But Jesus said over and over again that prosperity is not necessarily a sign of goodness. Wealth is not an indication that we are living for God. As a matter of fact, wealth may be a barrier to eternal life.

The majority of Christians in this generation and in all generations have not been wealthy people. Many of them have been poor *because* they were Christians. As this young man made his departure, Jesus said sorrowfully, "How hardly shall they that have riches enter into the kingdom of God! It is easier for a camel to go through the eye of a needle, than for a rich man to enter into the kingdom of God" (Mark 10:24-25). I believe our Lord used this illustration in a very literal sense. The camel was the largest animal to be found in Palestine at that time and it is totally impossible to conceive of a camel going through the eye of a needle. It is absurd.

Now we need to substitute the word "things" for the word "riches." I need to ask myself, "What is my camel?" The camel is different with each person. In some cases it is in fact wealth. In others it is talent or people or profession. The point is that whatever my camel's name may be, it is a barrier to the kingdom. Jesus is not saying that in some cases we may keep these things and squeeze through the eye of the needle. What he is saying is that if these things are a barrier between us and God, we must forsake them, abandon them completely, or else we will never have eternal life. It cannot be Jesus and our intellect, Jesus and our talent, Jesus and some other person, or Jesus and our profession. It must be Jesus only. This is the message of the rich young ruler.

And they came to Jerusalem: and Jesus went into the temple, and began to cast out them that sold and bought in the temple, and overthrew the tables of the moneychangers, and the seats of them that sold doves; And would not suffer that any man should carry any vessel through the temple. And he taught, saying unto them, "Is it not written, My house shall be called of all nations the house of prayer? but ye have made it a den of thieves." And the scribes and the chief priests heard it, and sought how they might destroy him: for they feared him, because all the people was astonished at his doctrine. And when even was come, he went out of the city.

Mark 11:15-19

Chapter 11

A Shortcut That Leads to Nowhere

The story of the cleansing of the temple is an example of a shortcut that people take from point A to point B—point A being a place or a situation in which we do not want to be and point B being a place or a situation to which we wish to go. Jesus cleansed the temple twice—once at the beginning of his ministry and once during the last week of his ministry. John tells the story of the first cleansing (John 2:13-17). Matthew, Mark and Luke tell the story of the second cleansing.

Our church in Toronto is situated on the corner of two streets—Sheppard Avenue and Wilfred. Once in a while someone will try to avoid going around that corner by cutting into our parking lot from Sheppard Avenue, going around the back of the church and coming out on Wilfred. They use the church as a shortcut. This is what people were doing in the days of Jesus with the temple area in Jerusalem. They literally used it as a shortcut to get from one part of Jerusalem to another.

We opened the doors of our new church building on Sunday,

October 28, 1962, but long before that our congregation went to the property in order to dedicate it to God. It was a rather dull day, but nearly three thousand people came for the ground-breaking service. On that occasion I reminded our people of God's promise to Joshua before the children of Israel entered the Promised Land. God said, "Every place that the sole of your feet shall tread upon, that have I given unto you, as I said unto Moses" (Josh. 1:3). Then I asked them to walk over every foot of that land and as they did so, to claim it for God by repeating over and over again these words: "God's land, God's land, God's land."

I suggested that as they did this they should remember the purpose for which this land was being dedicated. The gospel will be preached here. Children will be dedicated to God and educated in the Christian faith. Senior citizens will find comfort. The music of the gospel will be sung. Singles whose lives have been devastated by marital problems will be counselled. Money will be raised to evangelize the world. Prayer will be made for missionaries as well as for the sick, the lame, the halt and the blind. Christians will be edified by the preaching and teaching of the word of God. Some of them will leave this place and minister in foreign fields. Christian boys and girls will meet other Christian boys and girls and establish Christian homes. These six acres of land will be constantly busy in the service of God. This land is not designed to be a shortcut from Sheppard Avenue to Wilfred. It is dedicated to the service of God.

When King Solomon had finished the building of the temple, he assembled his people together to remind them of the purpose of the temple. This was to be the house of the Lord. It would be a holy place—the Ark and the Holy of Holies were in this place. It would also be a place where the people could confess their personal sin. Even if they were a long distance away from it, they could look in the direction of the temple while they confessed their sin. It would also be a place where they would be able to confess the sins of the nation. This was to be the place where they could ask God to help them in their battles against their enemies. It was here that they could come to ask for help in times of famine or catastrophe or plague. It would be a testimony to the rest of the world that God had always kept his promises to Israel. It would be a visible sign to the entire world that Jehovah is the true and living God. Finally, it would be a place where people from all over the world could come and pray. Most of these things were expressed in Solomon's prayer on the day of the dedication (1 Kings 8:31-53).

No wonder our Lord became indignant when he discovered the people of his day using the temple for their own convenience as a shortcut. The temple included a large area of the city of Jerusalem. Each of the four sides extended for approximately half a mile. (Sometime go out in your car and measure an area like that in your town. I think you will be amazed at the size of it.) The temple was walled, and there were a number of gates that served as entrances. The floor of the temple area was paved with marble. That was the court of the gentiles.

The actual temple building started about halfway north, that is, about four hundred and fifty yards from the southern entrance gate, or the length of four football fields. The building was surrounded by a wall that measured approximately four-and-a-half feet in height. There were signs on the wall written in both Greek and Latin that read, "Let no man of another nation enter inside the barrier and the fence around the temple. Whoever is caught will have himself to blame that his death follows." Gentiles were not permitted to go into the actual building, but they could come through the gates and worship God in the vast area outside the building.

King Solomon's temple had been built in 969 B.C., during the fourth year of his reign. It was finished seven years later in 962 B.C. That temple was destroyed by the Chaldeans in 586 B.C. In other words, Solomon's temple remained for something like 376 years. The people started to rebuild the temple about fifty years later, towards the end of their exile. The temple that they rebuilt was partially destroyed in 168 B.C. and even more in 54 B.C., but it was not completely destroyed.

It was on the remains of this partially destroyed temple that Herod the Great started building his temple in the year 19 B.C. It was finished after Herod's death, just before the year A.D. 70, when once again it was completely destroyed by the Romans. Herod's temple was almost totally new. He used what was left of the temple that had been destroyed in 54 B.C. so that there would be some continuity in the existence of the building. However, it was much more elaborate than the temple had ever been before. It might well have been one of the seven wonders of the ancient world. It was spectacular, dazzling, breathtaking, spellbinding. Apparently it would have been difficult to exaggerate the splendor of Herod's temple.

Some of the stones that were used measured sixty-seven feet by eight feet by nine feet. That would be the size of a large trailer truck. This is what one of his disciples was looking at when he said, "Master, see what manner of stones and what buildings are here!" And this is what amazed the disciples when our Lord answered, "Seest thou these great buildings? there shall not be left one stone upon another, that shall not be thrown down" (Mark 13:1-2). What army could possibly dislodge stones of this magnitude—to say nothing of doing so in such a complete manner that there would not be one left on top of another. This just could not happen, but it did—during the Roman destruction in A.D. 70.

The practice of buying and selling animals for sacrificial purposes and the changing of foreign currency probably started after the captivity and maybe not until the year A.D. 30. Before that the people brought their own animals or else bought them in some other part of the city, but by the time of our Lord this whole business had been brought right inside the temple walls. It is difficult to realize how serious this was unless we know a little bit about the vast number of sacrifices that were made. On the opening day of Solomon's temple he sacrificed 22,000 oxen and 128,000 sheep (1 Kings 8:63). And remember that Solomon's temple was not as large as Herod's. In the Passover of A.D. 66 the people used 256,500 lambs. The buying and selling of all of these animals was carried on inside the temple walls in the only place that the Gentiles could worship God.

Imagine the sounds and smells of that courtyard! Not only was there a certain amount of desecration as a result of that enormous number of animals being there, but they were sold at very high prices. Pigeons that on the outside might cost approximately five cents were sold inside the walls for as much as four dollars and ten cents. There was also a temple tax that had to be paid in Jewish coins. This is what gave rise to the money-changers. Jews came from all over the world bringing with them Greek, Roman, Egyptian and other kinds of coins. The money-changers took these foreign coins and exchanged them for Jewish coins. This was also done at a very high rate of interest. The exchange alone amounted to approximately 45,000 dollars per year. The temple tax came to the grand figure of at least 372,000 dollars per year. When the Roman consul Marcus Crassus plundered the temple in the year 54 B.C., he took out something like ten or twelve million dollars in cash.

What incensed Jesus the most was the fact that all of this corrupt business was going on in the only area of the temple that Gentiles were permitted to worship—the Gentiles' Court. Not only had the temple area become a shortcut by which people moved from one area of Jerusalem to another, but the religious leaders of the day were using it to make a great deal of money at the expense of the poor people who wished to make sacrifices.

The temple today is the Christian church—that is, the living body of Christ. That is what the apostle Paul was referring to when he wrote to the Corinthians: "What? know ye not that your body is the temple of the Holy Ghost which is in you, which ye have of God, and ye are not your own?" (1 Cor. 6:19). It is important that we treat the temple of God, the church, as it should be treated. The church is not a shortcut to respectability and prosperity. We do not accept Jesus Christ as our Savior and join the church so that we may prosper personally in this world.

In the days of Jeremiah the people used the temple as a sort of badge of merit. They went about, says Jeremiah, crying out to everybody, "The temple of the Lord, the temple of the Lord" (Jer. 7:4). They hoped that their connection with the temple would hide their sin. Jeremiah knew better than that, and he told them in so many words that they were robbers, murderers, adulterers, blasphemers and idolaters. What they needed was not to proclaim loudly their connection with the temple of the Lord. They needed to amend their ways and their doings (Jer. 7:5).

Men and women have not changed a great deal over the centuries. In the Old Testament they used the temple to gain their respectability. In our day many people use the church for the same reason. I think if Jeremiah were to speak to us today he might say, "Why do you continually cry out, 'The Church! the church! the church!' Why don't you change your way? Why don't you get right with God?"

Sometimes we use the church for our personal profit. Very often we have joined it in order to make better social contacts or business contacts, and we seem to have forgotten that the primary purpose of the church is that it is a place to contact God.

We're concerned with those areas of church work that help us or our families. We are happy to give and pray and work for anything that affects us and our families. We are quite willing to sink a great deal money into the building of new buildings. We are eager for the church to start clubs and organizations that will be helpful to our own family and we seem to have forgotten that, like the Court of the Gentiles in the old Jewish temple, the church is the only place through which the people of the world can meet God. If they do not meet God as a result of their associations with the body of Christ—the church, then they will go into eternity without ever having had a chance.

That is why both in our personal lives and in the lives of our local churches we must make sure that the majority of our money and our prayer and our effort is not spent on ourselves and our families but on people and projects that are concentrating upon reaching the world with the gospel of Jesus Christ. The old motto is very true: "The light that shines farthest shines brightest nearest home." If we concentrate on beaming our light to the lost peoples of the world, we will never have to suffer from lack of light in the work at home. However, it is possible for our light to be extremely brilliant in and around the home base and yet not be reaching out to the back rows of the world. There are still people in our world who have not had the opportunity of hearing the gospel for the first time: "Why should any one hear the gospel twice before everyone has heard the gospel once?"

And Jesus sat over against the treasury, and beheld how the people cast money into the treasury: and many that were rich cast in much. And there came a certain poor widow, and she threw in two mites, which make a farthing. And he called unto him his disciples, and saith unto them, "Verily I say unto you, That this poor widow hath cast more in, than all they which have cast into the treasury: For all they did cast in of their abundance; but she of her want did cast in all that she had, even all her living."

Mark 12:41-44

Chapter 12

A Recklessness That Pleases God

The most intriguing part of this chapter is the story of the widow who gave everything she had. Mark takes only four verses right at the end of the chapter to tell it, but its significance cannot be overstated. It took place on the Tuesday of the last week of our Lord's ministry in this world before he went to the cross.

By way of recapitulation we should remember that on Sunday, by our calendar, Jesus and his disciples had come from Jericho to Bethany, a distance of about fifteen miles. Jesus waited here with ten of the disciples while two of them went into the village to borrow a colt which he was about to ride into Jerusalem. On this occasion he made a victorious entry into the city, went to the temple and looked at it, then returned to Bethany for the night.

The next day, Monday, he returned once again to Jerusalem and on his way he cursed the fig tree that was bearing no fruit. Then once again he entered the temple, where he cast out the money-changers who were doing their corrupt business in the Court of the Gentiles. Again he returned to Bethany for the night (Matt. 21:7).

On Tuesday of that same week he returned to Jerusalem with his disciples, and as they passed the cursed fig tree, they saw that it had dried up. They proceeded into the temple, where our Lord had an extremely long discussion with the priests, the scribes, the elders and the Pharisees. In his Gospel, Mark devotes forty-seven verses to this discussion—seven of them in chapter eleven and forty in chapter twelve.

We do not know exactly which gate of the temple Jesus and his disciples used on this occasion, but perhaps they went through the south gate. In making their way to the actual building of the temple, they would have to walk north across the Court of the Gentiles—where he had cleansed the temple on Monday—a distance of more than four football fields before they came to the small wall that surrounded the building itself. They went through one of the gates in that wall where only Jews were allowed to go. They would climb a terrace that consisted of fourteen steps, and that would take them into the Court of the Women. Only Jewish men could go beyond this vast area.

The Court of the Women was large—approximately eighty thousand square feet. Our auditorium in The Peoples Church is large enough to comfortably seat two thousand people and its area is only 54,232 square feet. There was room enough in the Court of the Women for more than three thousand people to worship.

Along the walls of this court there were thirteen trumpet-shaped collection receptacles into which the people put their offerings. These receptacles were placed in such a way that the wide part was on the floor and the narrow part extended upwards. They would be identified by some name that indicated what the offerings that were put into that particular receptacle were going to be used for. One of them might be for the general expenses of the temple—corn, oil, wine, and incense for the daily sacrifices. There would be another of these trumpets where the people could pay their temple tax, and perhaps one that was designated to receive money to help the poor. This area was referred to as the treasury, and it was here that Jesus sat while he watched the people making their offerings.

He observed that the middle-class and wealthy people gave substantially. Then came a woman who was a very poor widow, and what she put into the receptacle was so small that it didn't even make a noise when it fell. It is described in the Bible as two mites. A mite was a small copper coin or a *lepta*—a word that means a thin coin. In our monetary system we have no coin that is as small in its value as this mite. Apparently our

Lord was not impressed by the gifts of the affluent people—gifts that probably made a considerable noise when they were dropped into the receptacles. However, when he saw the widow give her very small offering, he was so impressed that he called his disciples over to teach them something about giving: "Verily I say unto you, That this poor widow has cast more in, than all they which have cast in the treasury" (Mark 12:43).

It is interesting to notice the occasions in this Gospel alone when the expression about *calling his disciples to him* is used in connection with an extremely important event or announcement. One of these was when he actually called the twelve men who would follow him and become his disciples: "And he goeth up into a mountain, and calleth unto him whom he would: and they came unto him. And he ordained twelve, that they should be with him, and that he might send them forth to preach" (Mark 3:13-14).

It occurs again when he sent his disciples out two by two: "And he called unto him the twelve, and began to send them forth by two and two; and gave them power over unclean spirits" (Mark 6:7).

Once more we find it when Jesus is about to feed the four thousand people: "In those days the multitude being very great, and having nothing to eat, Jesus called his disciples unto him, and saith unto them, I have compassion on the multitude, because they have now been with me three days, and have nothing to eat" (Mark 8:1-2).

One of the most important occasions when this phrase occurs is after the apostle Peter's confession that Jesus was indeed the Christ: "And when he had called the people unto him with his disciples also, he saith unto them, Whosoever will come after me, let him deny himself, and take up his cross, and follow me" (Mark 8:34). Then follows Jesus' teaching that he would have to die and that those that followed him would have to suffer and might also have to die.

Another important part of Jesus' teaching was that greatness in the kingdom of God would be measured in terms of service. Again we find this expression: "But Jesus called them to him, and saith unto them, Ye know that they which are accounted to rule over the Gentiles exercise lordship over them; and their great ones exercise authority upon them. But so shall it not be among you: But whosoever will be great among you, shall be your minister" (Mark 10:42-43).

This is the expression that Mark used again when he told the story of the poor widow. Obviously he was about to demonstrate an important truth.

Adding even more importance to this occasion is the fact that Jesus introduced his teaching by using the word *Verily*. This is a translation of the Hebrew word Amen—a word that is also used in the New Testament. It means "as surely as God lives." Sometimes it was used as one of God's names or to describe God. Isaiah used it in this way: "He who blesseth himself in earth shall bless himself in the God of truth" (Isa. 65:16). The Hebrew word that is translated by the English word *truth* is *amen*.

It is also used in the last book of the Bible as one of the names of Jesus: "And unto the angel of the church of the Laodiceans write; These things saith the Amen, the faithful and true witness, the beginning of creation of God" (Rev. 3:14). If we were to put together all of the information that was introduced by the word *verily* it would include everything that Jesus taught. We would have a complete Christology in these passages. It precedes our Lord's comments about the sacrificial gift of the poor widow and gives a significance and importance to this incident.

So that we do not make the mistake of losing this story in biblical history, we should bear in mind the fact that Jesus still "sits over against the treasury" watching, listening and knowing. There is nothing in the Bible that is emphasized more than the fact that God the Father, God the Son, and God the Holy Spirit are totally aware of everything that has ever happened, everything that is happening now and everything that will happen throughout the rest of eternity. "Neither is there any creature that is not manifest in his sight: but all things are naked and opened unto the eyes of him with whom we have to do" (Heb. 4:13). The New International Version is probably better at this point: "Before the eyes of him to whom we must give an account."

The paraphrase of The Living Bible makes this verse even more apparent: "He knows about everyone, everywhere. Everything about us is bare and wide open to the all-seeing eyes of our living God; Nothing can be hidden from him to whom we must explain all that we have done."

In this sense God has always sat "over against the treasury": "And the Lord said, I have surely seen the affliction of my people which are in Egypt, and have heard their cry by reason of their taskmasters; for I know their sorrows" (Exod. 3:7).

The children of Israel in their Egyptian slavery had often thought that God had forgotten about them completely, that he was no longer concerned. They may have even thought that he had forsaken them and gone to some other group of people and that they were no longer the chosen race. When God spoke to Moses from the burning bush, he assured him that the people had not been forgotten, that he knew what was happening to them and that he still had a plan for them.

110

God was sitting "over against the treasury" when the people complained to Moses: "How long shall I bear with this evil congregation, which murmur against me? I have heard the murmurings of the children of Israel, which they murmur against me" (Num. 14:27).

Moses had sent twelve men across the Jordan River to spy out the land. Ten of these men brought back a bad report. They admitted that the land did indeed flow with milk and honey, but they said that the cities were well fortified and that the inhabitants looked like giants as compared to themselves, who appeared as grasshoppers.

However, two of the spies, Joshua and Caleb, were confident that they could overcome the people in the land and occupy it: "If the Lord delight in us, then he will bring us into this land, and give it to us; a land which floweth with milk and honey. Only rebel not ye against the Lord, neither fear ye the people of the land; for they are bread for us: their defence is departed from them, and the Lord is with us: fear them not" (Num. 14:8-9).

When the people complained bitterly against the Lord, in all probability they thought that they had managed to get away with it, but God heard their murmuring and all of the people twenty years of age and upward paid an enormous price for it. None of them were allowed to cross the Jordan River and actually go into the land. They all died in the wilderness. The only ones whom God allowed to go into the land were Joshua and Caleb.

God sits "over against the treasury": "For the Lord thy God hath blessed thee in all the works of thy hand: he knoweth thy walking through this great wilderness: these forty years the Lord thy God hath been with thee; thou hast lacked nothing" (Deut. 2:7).

Many times the people had not been sure. There were times when they felt as if God had left them. All they could see were the troubles that seemed to surround them on every hand, and in doing so they forgot that God understood and was quite aware of what was going on.

Jesus reminds us that the Father still sits "over against the treasury": "Are not two sparrows sold for a farthing? and one of them shall not fall on the ground without your Father. But the very hairs of your head are all numbered. Fear ye not therefore, ye are of more value than many sparrows" (Matt. 10:29-31).

It is vitally important that we remember God—God the Father and God the Son and God the Holy Spirit—is constantly aware of all that is happening in this world both among the wicked and the righteous. He is watching, listening and knowing.

God Sees the Outside and the Inside

It is also of vital importance for us to understand that God does not see, hear and know as we do: "But the Lord said unto Samuel, Look not on his countenance, or on the height of his stature, because I have refused him: for the Lord seeth not as man seeth; for man looketh on the outward appearance, but the Lord looketh on the heart" (1 Sam. 16:7).

God had instructed the prophet Samuel to anoint the next king of the Jews. Samuel was to go to the home of a man by the name of Jesse, who had a number of sons. He was to look at them and choose the one who was to be the king. Samuel would understand in his heart which was the right boy the moment he saw him. After the first son had stood before Samuel, God had uttered the words that we have just quoted. Samuel was able to see that this was a very fine young man. He was conscious of his stature, of his dress, of his education. Samuel was able to observe all of the outward signs. It was then that God made it very clear to Samuel that he was more concerned with what was inside the man than he was with the way he appeared on the outside. Samuel was only able to see what was on the outside. However, God does not see as man sees. God looks at us from the inside, and there is a great difference in the results.

When Jesus scathingly accused the Pharisees of hypocrisy, he stressed exactly the same principle: "Woe unto you, scribes and Pharisees, hypocrites! for ye may clean the outside of the cup and of the platter, but within they are full of extortion and excess" (Matt. 23:25).

God Sees and Weighs Our Actions

Man is only able to observe an action. The Bible makes it clear that God not only observes an action but also weighs it: "Talk no more so exceeding proudly; let not arrogancy come out of your mouth: for the Lord is a God of knowledge, and by him actions are weighed" (1 Sam. 2:3).

This is illustrated once again in the story of Daniel and the writing on the wall. Belshazzar, the king, asked Daniel to interpret the meaning of the writing. Daniel's reply was clear, "This is the interpretation of the thing: MENE; God hath numbered thy kingdom, and finished it. TEKEL: Thou art weighed in the balances, and art found wanting. PERES; Thy kingdom is divided, and given to the Medes and Persians" (Dan. 5:26-28). God was able to see what the king and his people were doing—as could Daniel. But God not only saw, he also weighed the king's actions.

God Sees through the Power of His Spirit

In the year 537 B.C., when Zerubbabel returned with some of the people to start rebuilding the temple, he could see nothing but mountains of opposition in front of him; but in the eyes of God, the mountains were wiped out by the power that God knew there was in his Spirit. It was the prophet Zechariah who gave God's message to Zerubbabel: "Not by might, nor by power, but by my spirit, saith the Lord of hosts" (Zech. 4:6). Man sees the mountains of opposition. God sees the power of the Holy Spirit.

Man's Knowledge Is Childish to God

The psalmist expresses it beautifully: "Such knowledge is too wonderful for me; it is high, I cannot attain unto it" (Ps. 139:6).

Perhaps we could understand what David was saying if we were to compare the knowledge of a five-year-old child with the knowledge of Albert Einstein. The child knows a little bit about his immediate world. Einstein sees what the child sees, but he is also aware of some of the ramifications of the entire universe. Make a similar comparison between Albert Einstein and God. Einstein knows a great deal about the universe, but God knows the ramifications not only of Einstein's little universe, but of all the galaxies that are far beyond anything that the most brilliant mind of man has ever conceived. In the field of knowledge God is to Einstein what Einstein is to a five-year-old child. That is why the apostle Paul says: "The foolishness of God is wiser than men" (1 Cor. 1:25).

Light and Darkness Are the Same to God

Man can only see what is in the light, or within the range of his instruments, but to God light and darkness are the same. It makes no difference: "Yea, the darkness hideth not from thee; but the night shineth as the day: the darkness and the light are both alike to thee" (Ps. 138:12).

113

God Sees in the Light of Eternity

"Lord, thou has been our dwelling place in all generations. Before the mountains were brought forth, or ever thou hadst formed the earth and the world, even from everlasting to everlasting, thou art God" (Ps. 90:1-2).

"Jesus Christ the same yesterday, and today, and forever' (Heb. 13:8).

He who sits "over against the treasury" sees things as they relate to eternity—from everlasting (in the past) to everlasting (in the future). We know and hear and see only in terms of time. God knows and sees and hears in terms of eternity.

Now let's return to the scene in the temple. How did the disciples see it? They saw wealthy people as they came to the trumpet-shaped receptacles in the temple, putting in very large amounts of money. Some of it probably made a great deal of noise as it landed on the metallic surface.

I am sure that there were some "Amens" heard from people who were standing around and perhaps some of the disciples may have joined them. There might even have been an occasional "Hallelujah" when they heard a particularly large amount dropped in. These big gifts undoubtedly impressed the disciples, as they would have impressed us.

When the poor widow put in her two very thin coins, some of the disciples may not have noticed her at all. Her gift made almost no noise against the metal. Perhaps one of the disciples may have said, "That was a stupid thing to do. She should have kept it for herself. She cannot afford that kind of a gift." Certainly nobody said "Amen," and no one even thought about saying "Hallelujah."

Our Lord saw exactly the same scene, but as is always true with God, he was able to see what the disciples could not see. When the large gifts were put in by the wealthy people, our Lord did not even notice the size of the gifts. What he did see was the abundance that these people had left for themselves after they had made their gifts to God. When the widow dropped her extremely small gift into the treasury, our Lord did not notice the size of the gift at all. What he did notice was the fact that after she had made that gift, she would have nothing left. She had given what Jesus referred to as her "living"—that is, all that stood between her and death.

Jesus did not hear the loud clatter of the big gifts in the temple, but rather the silence in heaven because these people had given something that had not cost them anything. He heard—not the quiet tinkle of the

114

widow's gift in the temple—but the drum roll that was starting in heaven so that the angel choir could sing the "Hallelujah Chorus" because it cost that widow so much. It was all that she had.

The story of the widow's two mites was not about money but about sacrifice. Man sees the gift, but the one who sits "over against the treasury" sees the sacrifice. How much did it cost us to give our money, our time, our service, our talent? How much did it cost us to become a missionary or to become a pastor?

In the light of this story we might well ask the question: Who is the greatest pastor in the world? This would be a relatively easy question for us to answer. We would get a book that lists the ten most important churches in the world, the ten largest churches in the world, or those that had experienced the most church growth. We would find out who the pastors of those churches were and we would have the answer to our question.

Would it be Dr. Yongi Cho in that massive church in Korea—the largest church in the world? Would it be Jack Hyles in Hammond, Indiana—that church that has achieved such a miraculously large Sunday school attendance? Would it be Jerry Falwell in Lynchburg, Virginia—with that church that is now known throughout North America as a result of its vast television ministry? Would it be Jack MacArthur in Los Angeles—with that church that has put together two enormous Sunday morning services that are led by a Bible teacher without peer? Or perhaps would it be Paul Smith in Toronto, Canada—with the church that some people say may have done more for world missions than any other?

We rate our pastors by the size of their churches, the number of books they have written, the countries in which they have preached, the television stations on which their voice is heard and the amount their church gives to missions.

We measure our pastors by church growth: how many people did he win to Christ, how many did he baptize, how many of his young people have gone into full-time service.

However, he who sits "over against the treasury" rates pastors by how much it costs them. It is not the size but the sacrifice that Jesus sees. I think John Mark was very much aware of this biblical principle. If I were to be confronted by him today, I think he might ask questions that are quite different from our questions. How much has it cost you to serve Jesus Christ? Where are your scars? What have you done without? How much has it hurt you?

I think if my ministry were to be measured by the standards of the one who sits "over against the treasury," I might be looked upon as the rich people. Certainly I have given something, but it has been out of my abundance. I have served the Lord Jesus Christ, but I have done so in comparative personal comfort. Is there any real sense in which I could say, "I have denied myself. I have taken up my cross. And I have followed Jesus?"

Who is the greatest pastor in the world? He may be somebody who is totally unknown beyond his own immediate pastorate. He might be some fellow pastor of mine in the city of Toronto who has been faithful in a very small church in some obscure area of the city. However, he visits the sick. He spends time with the lonely. He cooks meals for the aged. He rides a bicycle, drives an old car, doesn't own his own home and dresses in threadbare suits. His name will never appear in print. His church will never be listed among the ten largest churches in North America. There will not be a huge crowd at his funeral. But he gave God everything he had. He paid the price. He bears the scars of the shepherd of a small flock.

If Paul Smith and that man were in the temple in the days of the Lord and Jesus was sitting "over against the treasury," what would he see? Remember: It's not how big the contribution—it's how much did it cost.

Let's ask another question in the light of this story. Who is the greatest church member in the world? Or who is the most important member in my Sunday morning audience, or anyone's Sunday morning audience?

The important thing is not that he is there—in the Sunday morning service. But how much did it cost him to be there. Many "Christians" are too tired to go to church on Sunday morning. Many cannot worship God on Sunday because it's the only day they have to rest, to work in the garden or to do the laundry.

Here is a Christian who is there, in his place, ready to worship God. But is he willing to give up anything to return on Sunday night? Of course, there are a great many more reasons why Christians must stay home on Sunday night than there are reasons to stay home on Sunday morning. Is the church member who is in his place on Sunday morning interested enough in the service of God to come back at all on Sunday night? Certainly, the Sunday-morning-only kind of Christian cannot weigh very much in the eyes of the Savior.

But then let's ask another question in our search for the most important church member: Is he concerned enough about the service of God to become involved in some activity in the church that is going to demand some of his time and energy on a regular basis? The real burden of most of our churches is carried on the shoulders of about ten percent of the church membership. These are the people that are willing to obligate themselves to a Sunday school class that demands their regular attendance and study and faithfulness. They are the members who will allow themselves to be obligated to sing in a choir, where they will have to be there for a practice regularly on one of the week nights as well as turning up at both of the services on Sunday. These are the people that join Evangelism Explosion or any one of a number of things that the church is attempting to do to edify the saints and to reach out to the unbelievers.

The greatest church member is that man or woman who has been willing to give up a great deal of his own time and energy and talent in his service for the Lord. That is the most important church member—not the wealthiest, but the one whose service cost him personally the most.

Becoming a Christian is not simply a matter of saying, "Here I am Lord! Save me from hell and get me to heaven." Becoming a Christian involves another sort of commitment: "Here I am Lord! Forgive me for my sin. Thank you for giving your life for me. There is no way I can even begin to pay you back, but I'm going to deny myself, and take up my cross and follow you. From here on in with me it is going to be anything, anytime, and anywhere."

There has to be a reckless abandonment, a risk, if we are to be of any real value to Jesus Christ.

It was a thrilling moment in The Peoples Church on Sunday, May 9, 1976, when I was able to announce to our congregation that for the first time our world missions giving exceeded one million dollars. I can remember rather deliberately announcing the specific amount— $1,132,672! When I made this announcement, our minister of music raised his baton. There was a rumble of drums, then the choir and orchestra burst forth in that glorious song of praise, the "Hallelujah Chorus."

Sometimes I wonder if God is very much impressed by this rather large amount of money for world missions. Almost every week I receive letters from our television audience that read something like this: "How I wish I could give more! I realize how great the need is but here is five dollars. I hope it will be of some help.

"I am eighty-six years of age. My health is bad. I am living alone on a very small pension. I am a widow." And then she apologizes to me because she is unable to do as much as she wants to do.

I unfold that tightly wrapped five-dollar bill which she has been keeping in a secure place, and I realize that she really needs it herself. I know that for a few days she will eat a little less, until her government cheque comes in. It seems to me that somewhere close to the throne of God I can hear a drum roll in heaven. The four living creatures and the twenty-four elders and the redeemed of all ages and myriads of angels are poised to sing the "Hallelujah Chorus."

I look again at the five-dollar bill that was sent to me by the widow who could not really afford it. But now I see it through the eyes of Jesus, who sits "over against the treasury," and now I see it as a million-dollar bill! I can hear him saying, "Verily I say unto you, that this poor widow hath cast more in than they all . . . for they gave of their abundance; but she of her want did cast in all that she had, even her living."

Part Five

Ingredients in Life - Not Signs—Chapter 13
Impulsive Love - Not Calculated—Chapter 14
Political Career - Not Sound Judgment—Chapter 15

And as he went out of the Temple, one of his disciples saith unto him, "Master, see what manner of stones and what buildings are here!" And Jesus answering said unto him, "Seest thou these great buildings? there shall not be left one stone upon another, that shall not be thrown down. And as he sat upon the mount of Olives over against the temple, Peter and James and John and Andrew asked him privately, "Tell us, when shall these things be? and what shall be the sign when all these things shall be fulfilled?" And Jesus answering them began to say, "Take heed lest any man deceive you."

Mark 13:1-5

Chapter 13

Ingredients In Life—Not Signs

The brilliance and glory of the Jewish temple in Jerusalem would make any of the seven wonders of the ancient world pale into mediocrity.

Certainly, the Hanging Gardens of Babylon were beautiful almost beyond description. They were built by Nebuchadnezzar in the first half of the fifth century B.C. It was said that he built them for his wife, who had come from a part of the world where the growth was luxurious, and she could not stand the desert-like territory surrounding the city of Babylon. However, they could hardly have been put into the same class as the Jewish temple.

And about the same time the king of Lydia built the Temple of Diana in the city of Ephesus. Actually he never finished it because it took a hundred and twenty years to be completed. It covered two acres of ground and boasted one hundred columns. Diana, or Artemis, was the Greek goddess of wild animals, vegetation, chastity, childbirth and the hunt. However, the Temple of Diana would have lost a great deal of its brilliance if it had been erected alongside of the Jewish temple.

The Statue of Zeus, king of the gods, was built to celebrate the first Olympic games. It was thirty feet high, made primarily of gold and ivory. The image of Zeus was sitting on a throne with a victory image in his right hand and a sceptre with an eagle on it in his left hand. It was remarkable, but hardly in the same category as the Jewish Temple.

The Mausoleum of Halicarnassus was the tomb of Mausolus, who had been the ruler of the Greek city-state of Halicarnassus. It was built in the year 353 B.C. by Artemisia, the woman who had been his sister and also his wife, but it was only a beautiful burial place—not to be compared with the Jewish temple.

The island of Rhodes was in the Aegean Sea near the Turkish coast. It boasted a statue of Helias the sun-god which was called the Colossus of Rhodes. It was a gigantic statue—one hundred feet high, built towards the end of the second century B.C., undoubtedly one of the seven wonders of the ancient world—that is, if one had never seen the Jewish temple.

The Pharos Lighthouse in Alexandria, Egypt, probably gained its historic fame from the fact that it was the first lighthouse—at least the first one of any size. It was four hundred and forty feet high and its light was created by a blazing woodfire. This was indeed a remarkable accomplishment in the year 280 B.C., but I think if it had not been the first lighthouse that the world had ever seen, it would never have been numbered among the seven wonders.

The oldest of the seven wonders of the ancient world are the only ones that can still be seen today—the pyramids of Egypt. They were built some eleven hundred years before the time that the Jews were slaves in the land of Egypt. The base of one of the large pyramids would have covered eight football fields and risen to the height of a forty-story skyscraper. It contained two million, three hundred thousand blocks of stone, averaging about two-and-a-half tons each. The pyramids of Egypt were certainly a wonder—in size if in nothing else. They were even more remarkable when one considers the time in which they were built and the fact that most of the work was done by human muscle. The seven wonders of the ancient world were indeed breathtaking—each of them in at least one or two respects, but the Jewish temple in Jerusalem was a combination of wonders in many different respects.

Alfred Edersheim was a Jewish Christian who was a professor in Oxford University. He lived in the nineteenth century and is considered one of the authorities on the life of Jesus. His book *The Life and Times of Jesus the Messiah* is in almost every minister's library. Edersheim described the Jewish temple as follows:

A sanctuary of shining marble and glittering gold. When the pilgrims' feet stood within the gates of Jerusalem his one all-engrossing thought would be the Temple. As the pilgrim ascended the mount, crested by the symmetrical proportioned building, which could hold within its gigantic girdle not fewer than 210,000 persons, his wonder might well increase at every step. The mount itself seemed like an island, abruptly rising from deep valleys, surrounded by a sea of walls, palaces, streets, and houses, and crowned by a mass of snowy marble and glittering gold, rising terrace upon terrace. Altogether it measured about a thousand feet.

At its northwestern angle, and connected with it, frowned the Castle of Antonio, held by the Roman garrison. The lofty walls were pierced by massive gates—the unused gate (Tedi) on the north; the Susa Gate on the east, and the two Huldah Gates, and finally four gates on the west.

Within the gates ran all around covered double colonnades. Entering from the Xystus Bridge, and under the Tower of John, one would pass along the southern colonnade to its eastern extremity, over which another tower rose, probably the pinnacle of the history of the Temple. From this height yawned the Kedron Valley 450 feet beneath. From the lofty pinnacle the priest each morning watched and announced the earliest streak of day.

Passing out of these colonnades or porches you entered the Court of the Gentiles. Here must have been the market for the sale of sacrificial animals, the tables of the money changers, and places for the sale of other needful articles. [Remember, this was a huge area. In Solomon's Temple, which was much smaller, he sacrificed 22,000 oxen and 120,000 sheep on the day the Temple was opened. In the Passover of A.D. 66, in the larger Temple of Herod the Great, they sacrificed 256,500 lambs.] [1]

Certainly, neither labor nor money had been spared on the Temple. A thousand vehicles carried up the stone; ten thousand workmen under the guidance of a thousand priests, brought all of the costly material gathered into the house, of which Jewish tradition could say, "He that hath not seen the Temple of Herod, has never known what beauty is."

Flavius Josephus was almost a contemporary of Jesus. In fact, he may have been born a year or two before Jesus died. He was a Pharisee who lived to see the fall of Jerusalem. He was friendly to the Roman government and wrote a great deal about the history of the Jews. He too described the Jewish Temple:

Herod the Great got ready a thousand wagons, that were to bring stones for the building, and chose out ten thousand of the most skillful workmen, and brought a thousand sacerdotal garments for as many of the priests, and had some of them taught the arts of stonecutters, and others of carpenters, and then began to build.

There was a large wall to both the cloisters; which wall was itself the most prodigious work that was ever heard of by man. The cloister had pillars that stood in four rows one over against the other all along, for the fourth row was inter-woven into the wall, which also was built of stone; and the thickness of each pillar was such that three men might, with their arms extended, fathom it around, and join their hands again, while its length was twenty-seven feet, with a double spiral at its base; and the number of all the pillars in that court was 162.

The wall at the front was adorned with beams, resting upon pillars, that were inter-woven into it, and that front was all of polished stone, insomuch that its fineness, to such as had not seen it was incredible, and to such as had seen it, was greatly amazing.[2]

The original Temple that was built by King Solomon was considerably smaller than the Temple built by Herod the Great. However, the materials that King David gathered together so that Solomon could proceed with the Temple were breathtaking—6,600,000 pounds of gold, 66,000,000 pounds of silver and so much brass and iron that they did not bother to count it (1 Chron. 22:14).

Most of the carvings, sculptures and instruments were made of gold and silver—some of bronze. Among these were such things as flowers, pomegranates, palm trees, oxen, lions, chariots, cherubims, lamps, tables, chains, doors, pillars, altars, bowls, candlesticks, spoons, censors, cups, tongs, etc. In some areas even the nails that were used were made of gold.

The disciples were obviously overawed at the beauty of the Temple: "And as he went out of the temple, one of his disciples saith unto him, Master, see what manner of stones and what buildings are here!" (Mark 13:1). In the modern world they would have said, "What stones! What buildings! Wow!" But all of this glory was to be short-lived. The Temple was to be completely destroyed. Jesus prophesied that this would happen: "Seest thou these great buildings? there shall not be left one stone upon another, that shall not be thrown down" (Mark 13:2). Within a very short time after Jesus made this prophesy, it was literally fulfilled. The Roman emperor Titus destroyed Jerusalem and the Temple completely in the year A.D. 70. It was burned and then methodically taken apart stone by stone—probably in search of gold that may have been put between the stones to give it greater stability. Titus was a Roman general at the time and became emperor nine years later, in A.D. 79.

It was this prediction about the destruction of the Temple that led the disciples to ask Jesus about the future. The account that is given in the Gospel of Mark would lead us to believe that they were simply asking Jesus about the Temple and when it would be destroyed: "Tell us, when shall these things be? and what shall be the sign when all these things shall be fulfilled?'' (Mark 13:4).

Matthew makes it clear that they were not only asking Jesus about the destruction of the Temple, but the end of all things, in particular, about the time of his Second Coming: "Tell us, when shall these things be? And what shall be the sign of thy coming, and of the end of the world?''(Matt. 24:3).

Sometimes we make the mistake of thinking that in our Lord's answer to this question he is giving us a list of the various things that will happen before the Second Coming—signs that the Second Coming is near or about to happen. Actually, these are not signs at all. They are things that happen in the world that are common to most generations—both during the time when Jesus was speaking and in almost every century afterward.

1. False Christs

"For many shall come in my name, saying, I am Christ; and shall deceive many" (Mark 13:6). Christian people have always been natural candidates for false teachers. Generally we are fed up with world conditions and we would like to find easy answers. False teachers very seldom gain their followers from unbelievers. They prey upon the church, and there is a very real sense in which they fulfil the picture of the false "christs" that Jesus predicted. It is true that there will be a final Anti-Christ but in every century there have been deceivers. What Jesus is saying here is that these events are not a sign that the Second Coming is close, but rather, they are an ingredient of life in every century.

2. Wars—Actual and Threatening

"And when ye shall hear of wars and rumors of wars, be ye not troubled: for such things must needs be; but the end shall not be yet" (Mark 13:7). When Jesus made this prediction, the Roman Empire was in a state of comparative peace after over one hundred years of civil war. Augustus Caesar had become emperor in the year 27 B.C. and was still living when Jesus was born. The "Augustan Age" has always been considered the golden age of Roman literature, architecture, building and expansion. Jesus is telling his disciples that they should not expect this period of peace to go on forever. There will be wars, both actual and threatened. But these are not the sign of the Second Coming. Rather, this is one more of the ingredients of life in this world in any century.

3. Persecution

"But take heed to yourselves: for they shall deliver you up to councils; and in the synogogues ye shall be beaten: and ye shall be brought before rulers and kings for my sake, for a testimony against them" (Mark 13:9).

Jesus warns the disciples that they may expect persecution not only from the secular rulers of the world but also from the religious leaders and even from members of their own families.

The point here is that they will suffer because they are Christians—"for my sake." Because you are my followers, because you bear my name, because you preach my gospel, because you teach my doctrine and because you promote my cause, you will be persecuted.

When the disciples were beaten in the first century, they were very conscious of the fact that the lash that was being laid upon them was really intended for Jesus. In that sense they were bearing the lash for him. The apostle Paul had been persecuting Christians before his conversion, but when he was confronted by Jesus on the Damascus Road, the Lord accused him of persecuting him. "Saul, Saul, why persecutest thou me? And he said, Who art thou, Lord? And the Lord said, I am Jesus whom thou persecutest" (Acts 9:4-5).

The same thing is reflected in Paul's letter to the church of Philippi. "For to you has been given the privilege not only of trusting him but also of suffering for him. We are in this fight together. You have seen me suffer for him in the past; and I am still in the midst of a great and terrible struggle now, as you know so well" (Phil. 1:29-30, The Living Bible).

Paul is not crying. Rather, he is rejoicing. The Christians in Philippi knew that Paul had been beaten when he was put into the Philippian jail, but every time he received a lash at the hands of the jailor, he rejoiced. Perhaps he showed his joy by saying the name of his Savior after each lash—"Jesus, Jesus, Jesus."

We do not know the actual song that he and Silas sang under those conditions, but perhaps if they had been alive today, they would have been singing some such chorus as

I'm so happy, here's the reason why;
Jesus took my burdens all away.

Stanton W. Gavitt

126

It is little wonder that Paul is able to say in this same epistle:

I count all things but loss for the excellency of the knowledge of Christ Jesus my Lord: for whom I have suffered the loss of all things, and do count them but dung, that I may win Christ, And be found in him, not having mine own righteousness, which is of the law, but that which is through the faith of Christ, the righteousness which is of God by faith: That I may know him, and the power of his resurrection, and the fellowship of his sufferings, being made conformable unto his death (Phil. 3:8-10).

This is what kept the Christians going in the first century. They were bearing the lash for Jesus. They had the unparalleled opportunity of bearing the blows that the world would have liked to have laid directly on the back of Jesus.

This is what kept William Tyndale going in the sixteenth century. After being kept in prison for more than a year and a half, he was brought out, tied to a stake, strangled by the hangman and burned. Tyndale was the brunt of this barbaric treatment only because he translated the Bible from Latin, a language which none of his people could understand, into English, the language that could talk to his people. His final words on earth were "Lord! Open the King of England's eyes."

This is also what sustained Nicholas Ridley and Hugh Latimer during the same period of murder by the Roman Catholic church. Both Ridley and Latimer were bishops of the church. Their crime was that they preached sermons and wrote against such things as purgatory, the immaculate conception of the Virgin Mary, the worship of images, etc. I have seen the place in Oxford where they were burned at the stake on October 17, 1555. They were both executed in the same place at the same time, only because they preached the gospel of Christ in a manner that was not acceptable to the Church of Rome. John Fox describes their murder vividly:

When they came to the stake, Mr. Ridley embraced Latimer fervently, and bid him: "Be of good heart, brother, for God will either assuage the fury of the flame, or else strengthen us to abide it."
A lighted faggot was now laid at Dr. Ridley's feet, which caused Mr. Latimer to say: "Be of good cheer, Ridley: and play the man. We shall this day, by God's grace, light up such a candle in England, as I trust, will never be put out."
When Dr. Ridley saw the fire flaming up towards him, he cried with a wonderful loud voice, "Lord, receive my spirit." Master Latimer, crying as vehemently on the other side, "O Father of heaven, receive my soul!"

received the flame as it were embracing of it. After that he had stroked his face with his hands, and as it were, bathed them a little in the fire, he soon died (as it appeareth) with very little pain or none.

Ridley and Latimer reflected the same joy and glory in bearing suffering for the Lord Jesus Christ as did the saints of the first century. They considered it a privilege.

The hymn writer A. H. Ackley, who will always be remembered for his great resurrection hymn "He Lives," wrote another hymn that is not as well known but expresses the idea of suffering for Jesus as one of the great privileges of the Christian life:

> I walked one day along a country road,
> And there a stranger journeyed, too,
> Bent low beneath the burden of his load:
> It was a cross, a cross I knew.

> I cried, "Lord Jesus," and he spoke my name;
> I saw his hands all bruised and torn;
> I stooped to kiss away the marks of shame,
> The shame for me that he had borne.

> "Oh let me bear thy cross, dear Lord," I cried,
> And, lo, a cross for me appeared,
> The one forgotten I had cast aside,
> The one so long, that I had feared.

> My cross I'll carry til the crown appears,
> The way I journey soon will end
> Where God himself shall wipe away all tears,
> And friend hold fellowship with friend.

> "Take up thy cross and follow me"
> I hear the blessed Savior call;
> How can I make a lesser sacrifice,
> When Jesus gave his all.

4. World Missions

"And the Gospel must first be published among all nations" (Mark 13:10).

The evangelization of the world is not a sign of the Second Coming, but rather a task that Jesus gave the church, that they must do between the destruction of Jerusalem and the Second Coming. World evangelization is an ingredient in the life of Christians in every century. The disciples thought that surely Christ would come back again shortly after Jerusalem had been destroyed. However, Jesus said that this was not the case. There was something that had to be done by the church before he could return. Everybody in the world had to hear the gospel. They had to know enough about Jesus Christ so that they could make an intelligent decision as to whether they would follow him or not, whether they would say yes or no, whether they would accept him as their Savior or not.

5. The Abomination of Desolation

"But when ye shall see the abomination of desolation, spoken of by Daniel the prophet, standing where it ought not, (let him that readeth understand,) then let them that be in Judaea flee to the mountains" (Mark 13:14).

Even the "abomination of desolation" is not a clear sign of the Second Coming because there have been other events that are in this class. In the year 168 B.C. Antiochus Epiphanes, the king of Persia, put a statue of Jupiter on the altar in the Temple. This, of course, was considered to be an abomination by the Jews. In Luke's record of this Olivet sermon he calls the destruction of Jerusalem a "desolation."

Certainly, it seems that there will be a final "abomination of desolation," but in itself an "abomination of desolation" is not a clear sign of the Second Coming, any more than the appearance of false Christs, wars and rumors of wars, persecution of Christians or the apparent completion of the task of world evangelization. The whole point of this passage is that there is no really clear sign that will tell us without any question whatsoever when Jesus is coming back again.

The message to the disciples is this: Don't jump to the conclusion that the end is just around the corner. Don't quit work, sit on the roof, detach yourselves from world affairs or set dates. Get set for the long haul. Endurance is the name of the game. These things may happen in every generation. All of them have happened before and all of them may happen again. They may be more severe in the last days, but on the other hand, they may not be any more severe.

The starvation that comes with the black horse in the Book of Revelation does not appear to me to be as bad as the starvation conditions that are in the world at the present time. If you have seen the starving people who stretch almost from the Atlantic Ocean to the Red Sea across the south of the Sahara Desert in Africa, it does not seem that the starvation that is described in the sixth chapter of the Book of Revelation is as severe. When the black horse comes into the world, it does not bring with it a state of total starvation by any means. There is wheat and barley to be bought. There is also oil and wine. True, it is selling at a high price, but in some of the countries in Africa there are areas where there is no food available at any price.

The message of Jesus in this chapter, and the parallel chapters in Matthew and Luke, is that there are no signs. Bad things happen, but they are ingredients in life during any of the centuries of world history. They are not peculiar to the last times. At the time of the Second Coming, life will be going on as usual: "as it was in the days of Noah . . . as it was in the days of Lot."

Even during the days of the great tribulation, life will go on more or less as usual. People will get married, babies will be born and some folk will die. The only dramatic sign comes almost simultaneously with the return of Christ—that is, the sign in the heavens: "But in those days, after that tribulation, the sun shall be darkened, and the moon shall not give her light, And the stars of heaven shall fall, and the powers that are in the heaven shall be shaken" (Mark 13:24-25).

But this is not really a sign either. It is a part of that climactic event—the Second Coming of Jesus Christ. The two are inseparable. It is an unusual combination of natural phenomenon, in which the elements seem to be getting together to cry out "Here He Comes!"

When the time does finally come, nothing about the Second Coming will be secret. Everybody will see it. Mark says, "And then shall they see the Son of man coming in the clouds with great power and glory" (Mark 13:26). He uses an unqualified "they"—that is, everybody.

Matthew says, "And then shall appear the sign of the Son of man in heaven: and then shall all the tribes of the earth mourn, and they shall see the Son of man coming in the clouds of heaven with power and great glory" (Matt. 24:30). Although Matthew uses a tribal type of grouping, he does not leave anybody out. And remember that by this time there will be no tribes of people anywhere in the world that will not have been evangelized. The task of world missions will have been completed. Every tribe will have heard. None will have been left out.

Luke joins Mark in using an unqualified "they": "And then shall they see the Son of man coming in a cloud with power and great glory" (Luke 21:27). "They"—none is left out. Everyone will see him.

John joins the other three gospel writers in emphasizing the total visibility of the Second Coming, but he does so in the Book of Revelation: "Behold, he cometh with clouds; and every eye shall see him, and they also which pierced him: and all kindreds of the earth shall wail because of him. Even so, Amen" (Rev. 1:7).

What a complete contrast this is to the obscurity of our Lord's first advent. At that time he came into the world as the baby of an unknown Jewish virgin in the little land of Palestine, which was an obscure province of the great Roman Empire. Jesus came to a stable, and the world of the vast Roman Empire carried on with business as usual. But not so the next time. The Second Coming of Christ will be an earth-shattering event. The concept of a secret coming is not to be found in the Bible.

The message of this chapter would not be complete if we did not notice the work of the angels at the time of the Second Coming: "And then shall he send his angels, and shall gather together his elect from the four winds, from the uttermost part of the earth to the uttermost part of heaven" (Mark 13:27).

The sad part of the Second Coming of Christ is the separation that takes place between the righteous and the unrighteous, God's people and the devil's people, those who have trusted Jesus Christ as their Savior and those who have not.

This is stressed throughout the gospels. "Let both grow together until the harvest: and in the time of harvest I will say to the reapers, Gather ye together first the tares, and bind them in bundles to burn them: but gather the wheat into my barn" (Matt. 13:30).

"One mightier than I cometh, . . . whose fan is in his hand, and he will thoroughly purge his floor, and will gather the wheat into his garner; but the chaff he will burn with fire unquenchable" (Luke 3:16-17).

"And beside all this, between us and you there is a great gulf fixed: so that they which would pass from hence to you cannot; neither can they pass to us, that would come from thence" (Luke 16:26).

"In that night there shall be two men in one bed; the one shall be taken, and the other shall be left. Two women shall be grinding together; the one shall be taken, the other left. Two men shall be in the field; the one shall be taken, and the other left" (Luke 17:34-36).

The entire twenty-fifth chapter of the Gospel of Matthew is about this division—the foolish virgins from the wise, the profitable servants from the unprofitable, and the sheep from the goats: "Then shall the King say unto them on his right hand, Come, ye blessed of my Father, inherit the kingdom prepared for you from the foundation of the world: Then shall he say also unto them on the left hand, Depart from me, ye cursed, into everlasting fire, prepared for the devil and his angels" (Matt. 25:34,41).

In the Old Testament days David knew about this division: "The Lord preserveth all them that love him: but all the wicked will he destroy" (Ps. 145:20).

The prophet Daniel was aware of this division: "And many of them that sleep in the dust of the earth shall awake, some to everlasting life, and some to shame and everlasting contempt." (Dan. 12:2).

"Blessed forever are all who are washing their robes, to have the right to enter in through the gates of the city, and to eat the fruit from the Tree of Life. Outside the city are those who have strayed away from God, and the sorcerers and the immoral and murderers and idolators, and all who love to lie, and do so. Their doom is the Lake that burns with fire and sulfur. This is the Second Death" (Revelation 22:14-15, 21:8, The Living Bible).

The Second Coming of Jesus Christ is glorious for God's people—the most glorious day of all time. The Second Coming is devastating for the wicked—it is God's payday.

> Have you counted the cost, if your soul should be lost,
> Though you gain the whole world for your own?
> Even now it may be, that the line you have crossed,
> Have you counted, have you counted the cost?

A.J. Hodge

Footnotes

1. Alfred Edersheim, *The Life and Times of Jesus the Messiah* (Grand Rapids, Michigan: W. B. Eerdmans Publishing Co., 1980) pp. 112, 120, 243, 244.
2. Flavius Josephus, _____, Vol. III, Book XV, Chapter XI (Grand Rapids, Michigan: Baker Book House, 1979), pp. 408, 409, 411.

And being in Bethany in the house of Simon the leper, as he sat at meat, there came a woman having an alabaster box of ointment of spikenard very precious; and she brake the box, and poured it on his head. And there were some that had indignation within themselves, and said, "Why was this waste of the ointment made? For it might have been sold for more than three hundred pence, and have been given to the poor." And they murmured against her. And Jesus said, "Let her alone; why trouble ye her? she hath wrought a good work on me."

Mark 14:3-6

Chapter 14

Impulsive Love—Not Calculated

Mary, Martha and Lazarus were anxious to do something for Jesus to express their gratitude for all that he had done for them—in particular, the raising of Lazarus from the dead. However, their own home was not large enough to take care of all the people they wished to invite, and so they asked another friend of Jesus—a man by the name of Simon—if they could have the dinner in his home. Simon had been a leper and had probably been healed by Jesus. Certainly at this time his leprosy was a thing of the past. Simon was overjoyed at the prospect of joining in this demonstration of gratitude to Jesus and he was glad to make his home available.

Jesus and his disciples were invited and, of course, Simon, Lazarus, Mary and Martha were also there, making a group of seventeen people—fifteen men and two women. There were probably others invited as well, but their names are not given.

During the course of the meal Mary did a rather unusual thing. Of

133

course she had joined with the others in arranging to have the dinner, but I suppose that she wanted to do something for Jesus that would express her own gratitude and love for all that the Savior meant to her. She broke open a very expensive bottle of perfume and poured it on Jesus as a sort of anointing. The perfume was in a very expensive alabaster bottle. Alabaster is an almost translucent, soft white stone that is very expensive. The perfume, spikenard, comes from a tree that grows in the Himalayan mountains—that great range that divides India from Tibet. With the primitive means of transport that were available in those days, it was extremely costly just to bring it the great distance between India and Palestine; but the perfume itself was very expensive apart from any transportation costs.

Some of the other guests objected to this outburst of Mary's devotion. They said that it was far too extravagant. The money could have been used for much more practical purposes.

The fourteenth chapter of Mark's gospel is a long one—seventy-two verses, and relates a great many very important things—the plans of Judas to betray Jesus, the arrangements that were made to have the Passover in the upper room, the Last Supper itself at which Jesus instituted the ordinance of the Lord's Supper, his prediction that Peter and all of the others would deny him, the agonizing prayer in the Garden of Gethsemene, the actual betrayal of Jesus by Judas, Jesus' trial before the high priest and, finally, Peter's denial.

By way of introduction to these extremely profound events in the life of our Lord, Mark pauses to tell this beautiful story about Mary's act of love. Jesus is about to enter into the work for which he came into the world. He is now going to "be about his Father's business" in earnest, but before he does so, he accepts this act of worship that stemmed from the heart of one of his closest disciples—Mary. When the others criticized her because of her extravagance, Jesus said: "Let her alone; why trouble ye her? she hath wrought a good work on me" (Mark 14:6).

There are two different Greek words that could have been used here that would have been accurately translated by our word *good*. One of them would have been the word *agathos* which means good—morally good. One could be good in this sense but also very stern, austere, unattractive or even obnoxious. In our Lord's story of the Pharisee and the publican who went to the Temple to pray, there is no doubt that the Pharisee could have been called a good man—that is, morally good, but there was nothing about him that was kind or gentle or gracious or lovely or beautiful. What the Pharisee was saying was, "God—you are looking at a righteous man. As an example of my righteousness you should know that I give tithes of all that I possess." And he was right. He was a morally good man.

The rich young ruler that Mark talks about in chapter ten was in almost the same category as the Pharisee—he was morally good. He was technically good. He had done the things that he should have done, but obviously, he had no heart for a hungry and dying world. He was not willing to give up his wealth in order to follow Jesus.

The other word that can also be translated by the word good is the Greek word *kalos*. *Kalos* also means morally good, but it is a goodness that is lovely, beautiful, attractive, winsome, delightful, charming or fragrant. This is the word that Jesus uses in this story. What Mary did was a lovely thing. It was a beautiful action. It was the same kind of goodness that was demonstrated by the Good Samaritan. What Mary did was a lovely thing to do and Jesus recognized it as such.

This kind of love has a certain extravagance about it. It has a lavish quality to it. It results in an action that is not calculated. There may even be a degree of recklessness connected with it that refuses to count the cost.

Most of us are familiar with this kind of love. We see it at Christmastime. Of course, we may spend our Christmas according to Scrooge. Then there is no evidence of this sort of love. Or, we may spend our Christmas according to Santa Claus. Then we will do some extravagant things on impulse—an impulse that comes from our hearts. All of us have gone through the experience of trying to decide what we should give to somebody who is very dear to us, like a mother. We have several things in mind and one of them is quite expensive. It costs a great deal more than we should really spend, but when we think of the person we love, we say, "Hey! It's for mother. Let's go for it!"

We do the same thing when we are planning a wedding for one of our daughters. I see people in my church doing this all the time. They have a wedding for their daughter that is really out of their class. They pay far too much for the wedding gown, much more than they should for the flowers and an exorbitant amount to one of the local hotels for the wedding dinner. When I see my people doing this, I have a tendency to say, "Why did they spend so much money. They certainly cannot afford it. It is far beyond their means."

But of course I know exactly why they did it. I did it myself for both my daughters. When we were making our plans, we said, "She's only going to get married once. She's our baby! Let's shoot the works!" You see, we did not have that kind of money, but we did have that kind of love.

Some of the ministries of our church are like this. There are some things that we do which cannot be worked out on a calculator. The questions how much does it cost and how much will it bring in are inadmissible. These are ministries and must be done from the heart without reference to the cost.

I am not suggesting that we should not be good stewards in our church work or that we should not be careful how we spend the Lord's money. I am not suggesting that the accountant with his calculator is not a very necessary person to have in every church. What I am saying is that there are some areas of work in every church that cannot be based on profit and loss. There are times when we must minister from the impulse of our hearts. There are times when we must break an expensive alabaster bottle full of perfume.

This is the way Jesus looked at Mary's act. He could not have cared less if it had been a widow's mite, worth almost nothing or a pound of perfume that was worth a fortune. He saw the act as an expression of love. In the eyes of Jesus, what Mary did was a beautiful thing.

We have the same response when our child brings something home from kindergarten. Perhaps he has made a valentine card for his mother or a birthday card for his father. We don't analyze it. We don't really see it. Certainly, we do not see it as it is. We see where it came from. We see the love in the little heart that created it, and when it is given to us, we say, "Fantastic! Wow! Hey, Mother, look at this!"

When we demonstrate this kind of love, we always run the risk of being misunderstood. Mary's action was completely misunderstood by those who were present. Mark says, "And there were some that had indignation within themselves, and said, Why was this waste of the ointment made?" (Mark 14:4). Mark uses the word *some*. He does not identify the critic. Matthew says: "But when his disciples saw it, they had indignation, saying, To what purpose is this waste?" (Matt. 26:8). Matthew identifies the critics as the disciples.

When John tells the story, he identifies the disciple as Judas Iscariot: "Then saith one of his disciples, Judas Iscariot, Simon's son, which should betray him, Why was not this ointment sold for three hundred pence, and given to the poor?" (John 12:4-5). It may be that Judas put the thought into the other disciples' minds, or he may have put into words what the rest of them were thinking about anyway. At any rate, he is the spokesman. They were thinking only in terms of money. The perfume must have been worth at least three hundred pence. That was more than one man's wages for an entire year. That was enough to feed three hundred families for one day.

136

They failed to see the spiritual significance of what Mary did. Maybe even Mary herself did not see the long-term value of her action. However, Jesus did, and he connected it with his death: "She is come aforehand to anoint my body to the burying" (Mark 14:8). Then Jesus added that the story of what Mary did that day would go with the gospel wherever it was taken throughout the entire world in the days that were ahead: "Verily I say unto you, Wheresoever this gospel shall be preached throughout the whole world, this also that she hath done shall be spoken of for a memorial of her" (Mark 14:9).

This is another of our Lord's sayings that would make it totally impossible for the disciples to think of the Second Coming as being imminent during their lifetime. The image here is one of the gospel moving gradually from country to country throughout the world. It must have been obvious to the disciples that this was not going to happen in a day or week or a month or even a year. They would have to have thought in terms of a number of years. If this was to have had any meaning at all, then there was no way that the Second Coming of Christ could have taken place at any moment immediately after his ascension. There had to be time for the gospel—and this story—to be carried throughout the world.

We can expect an impulsive act of love to be misconstrued by others. I'm sure that Mary was sufficiently mature to know this. She would have expected to be misunderstood by the Pharisees or by the doctors of the law or by the Sadducees or by the unbelievers. What must have been a shock to Mary was the fact that the criticism came from none of these outsiders, but rather from the disciples. That she did not expect.

I am sure that most of our modern "electronic evangelists" expect no end of criticism from the people of the world. When someone criticizes the television evangelists, the whole godless world climbs up on his bandwagon. I think this is no suprise to the evangelists. They expect it. Most of them know enough about the Bible to realize that if they do not receive any criticism from the world, they are probably not proclaiming the whole counsel of God. What hurts is when the church climbs up on the same bandwagon of criticism with the people of the world. It is vitally important that we are careful about whose bandwagon we choose to ride on. Of course, if there is a serious moral problem, we have an obligation to do something about it—much as we may not like to do it.

This *kalos* kind of love very often sees an opportunity that must be grasped or else will be lost: "For ye have the poor with you always, and whensoever ye will ye may do them good: but me ye have not always" (Mark 14:7).

We are being presented here not with a choice between Jesus and the poor but a choice between always and not always. Jesus is not suggesting that the poor should not be helped. He assumes that they do this on a regular basis, but he is pointing out the fact that their opportunities of doing something for him personally will soon be gone. As a matter of fact, at this particular time there was less than one week left when he would still be in the world and they would have an opportunity of ministering to him. After the ascension that opportunity would be gone forever.

Mary seemed to have this sixth sense that told her that this was an opportunity she could not put off until some other time. She instinctively knew that it was a case of now or never. There was no time to weigh the pros and cons. God loves a cheerful giver, not a careful giver.

How often it is that we stand beside some dear friend's casket and realize with an aching heart that it is now too late to do the things that we could have done just a few days earlier. "Why didn't I send her those flowers. Why didn't I go to the nursing home and visit him more often. Why didn't I make a special effort to apologize and get things straightened out between us. Why didn't I invite her over for dinner one more time. Why didn't I go ahead and tell her how much I loved her. Why? Why? Why?"

And now the chance is gone. We had the impulse but we did not act on it. I was ministering at a missionary conference in Philadelphia when I first heard about the famine conditions in Ethiopia. Tom Brokaw, the NBC anchorman for the evening news, was doing a special on it. I was deeply moved and thought that we should do something as a church to help feed these starving people.

I got on the telephone immediately, called my office and spoke to Wilfred Wright, our General Manager of Operations. "Let's clear the decks next Sunday and devote an entire hour on television to a telethon for Ethiopia."

It was an impulse. I didn't have time to look into the possibilities seriously. There were a thousand unanswered questions. But this was one of those things to which I felt impelled to respond even before I got all of the answers. We held the telethon and were able to send something in excess of $500,000 by way of World Relief Canada to help the suffering people of Ethiopia.

Others heard the same newscasts, were moved emotionally to the same extent and felt impelled to do something about it. However, they started to ask questions: "How can we be sure that the food will get there? Is there not a possibility that our money will be diverted and used for other purposes? Even if it does get there, the food may be left lying on the docks and it may rot before it gets to the people. The government of Ethiopia tends to be communistic. Surely we should not help a communistic government?"

These were all important questions and observations. But people were dying. They were starving to death. It was one of those opportunities to which we had to respond immediately or not respond at all. There was no time for questions. When people are starving to death, you do not ask them whether their government is communistic. You simply go ahead and feed them. They are human beings who need help.

We did eventually send people over to Ethiopia to follow-up the distribution of the food and to make sure that our money had been used wisely. We were grateful to God that there were no real problems. The money was getting through. The food was being distributed. Starving people were being helped.

When children are starving, you don't get out your calculator and work out all the fine details. You break your alabaster bottle. You demonstrate the kind of love Mary demonstrated when she poured the expensive perfume on Jesus. You break the alabaster bottle because if you do not do it now, there may never be another opportunity.

Judas was the man with the calculator, and when I preach on this story, I have a tendency to look around my congregation and wonder how many there are who are like Judas. I make the mistake of trying to find out how many Judases there are in my congregation. What I should be doing is looking into my own soul and asking the question, "How much of Judas is in me?" We have always had a tendency to put Judas in a class by himself. We put him in a special category. We think of him as diabolical, a fiend, a traitor, inhuman, etc. We don't even think about ourselves or talk about ourselves in the same breath. Judas has absolutely nothing to do with us.

Judas's besetting sin was materialism and greed. He thought that the kingdom was going to be built in the world during his lifetime. He became materialism and greed incarnate. He was materialism and greed personified.

What we forget is that the other disciples had some of these same characteristics. They too expected that the kingdom would be established in their lifetime. They wanted to know who would be the greatest in the kingdom, who would sit on Jesus' right hand and on his left.

Jesus tried to teach them that the kingdom would be characterized by service. It was to be a ministry. The kingdom was not to be a place from which they could cut out a chunk of material prosperity for themselves. It was to be a place into which they could put some of their own blood and sweat and tears. It was not to be a kingdom of getting. It was to be a kingdom of giving. Although Jesus said this to his disciples on a number of occasions, I do not really believe that they got the message until long after his resurrection and ascension.

From that day to this the church has had a tendency to think of the kingdom of God as something from which the members could make a personal profit. Perhaps in our day more than ever, this ugly creature is raising its head. Become a Christian and you will become affluent. Join the church and you will prosper. Love the Lord and he will reward you materially. Put your financial seed into the ground and he will multiply it in financial terms.

We have still to learn the lesson of the kingdom and what it is really all about, and as a result we try to build it by doing all the wrong things. The kingdom is not built by the accumulation of material things. The kingdom is not built by erecting one lavish building after another. The kingdom is not built by increasing the size of the crowds that we can draw to a Christian service. The kingdom is not built by increasing the number of television stations on which our program is heard. The kingdom is not built by the size of our budget or the eloquence of our sermons.

The kingdom is built by acts of love like Mary's. Jesus is more concerned about the lovely, attractive, beautiful, winsome, impulsive acts of love of our people than he is about the size of our budget—even our budget for the evangelization of the world. We need to go out and break some alabaster bottle in our communities. Of course, we will be criticized, we will be misunderstood, but Jesus delights in that impulsive heart that goes ahead and helps people without analyzing all the factors. Remember that some of the most important things that we have to do are like a harvest. If we do not bring it in now, the chance may go and be gone from us forever.

And straightway in the morning the chief priests held a consultation with the elders and scribes and the whole council, and bound Jesus, and carried him away, and delivered him to Pilate. And Pilate asked him, "Art thou the King of the Jews?" And he answering said unto him, "Thou sayest it." And the chief priests accused him of many things: but he answered nothing. And Pilate asked him again, saying, "Answerest thou nothing? behold how many things they witness against thee." But Jesus yet answered nothing; so that Pilate marvelled.

Mark 15:1-5

Chapter 15

Political Career—Not Sound Judgment

Nobody in his right mind wanted to represent the government in Palestine. Representing Rome in that explosive nation was more of a penalty than a privilege. Rome did not expect much, but it did want to keep the waters calm. If Pontius Pilate had released Jesus instead of Barabbas, he would have put an end to his political career and his chances of advance would have been gone. If Pilate had released Jesus, word would have got back to Rome rapidly and he would have been relieved of his position and never given another post again. Although he did not like the Jews at all, Pilate could not afford to offend the Jewish leaders. The Jews were a constant thorn in the flesh to Rome and all they wanted their representative to do was to keep a cover on the pot so that it would not boil over. Any other Roman in the same position would have done exactly what Pilate did.

Pilate, a stern man, was the fifth procurator of Judaea. He started to rule in A.D. 26 and continued for ten years—probably for a few years after Jesus had been executed. He had an army of some five thousand men with which to ensure the Roman occupation and he had the power of life and death over the people. The Jews could not have sentenced Jesus to death without the authority of Pilate. We know very little about the life of Pilate, but it is thought that when he returned to Rome after his ten years in Palestine, he committed suicide.

It is obvious that Pilate did not think the charges against Jesus were valid. He found no fault in him whatsoever. However, he gave in to the demands of the Jews because he was afraid of what Rome would do if he opposed them and caused an uprising.

Between the time Jesus was taken prisoner in the Garden of Gethsemene and the time he was brought before Pilate, he went through an excruciating, exhausting experience. There is little doubt that he had no sleep whatever. As closely as we can follow his movements, they were as follows:

1. He was taken from the Garden of Gethsemane directly to the home of Annas, who had been the former high priest. Although Annas was not the high priest at this time, he still had a great deal of influence and the other religious leaders thought they could do nothing without his consent (John 18:13).

2. He was taken from the home of Annas to the home of Caiaphas, who was the current high priest (John 18:34).

3. He was taken from the home of Caiaphas to be tried by Pilate. This was at about six o'clock in the morning (Mark 15:1).

4. Pilate questioned him briefly and then when he learned that he belonged to Herod's jurisdiction, he sent him to Herod (Luke 23:7).

5. Herod questioned him briefly and then attempted to demean him by putting a royal robe on him. Then he sent him back to Pilate (Luke 23:11).

6. Pilate's soldiers took him inside the common hall of the Praetorium, which is where they put the crown of thorns on him (Mark 15:16).

7. After a considerable amount of abuse and demeaning by the soldiers, Pilate brought Jesus back outside the Praetorium to the crowd. Jesus was still wearing the purple robe and the crown of

thorns. It was at this time that Pilate told the people that he could find no fault in Jesus, and when he presented Jesus to them, he said, "Behold the man!" (John 19:5).

8. Pilate then took Jesus back inside the Praetorium and questioned him further (John 19:9).

9. At last Pilate took Jesus back outside before the people and said, "Behold your king!" (John 19:13-14).

10. Pilate delivered Jesus to the people and he was led away to be crucified (John 19:16-17).

This gives us some idea of how totally exhausted Jesus must have been before he even headed for the cross. There had been no sleep or even rest. It was a continual process of questioning, buffeting, belittling and movement from one place another. It is little wonder that he did not have enough strength left to carry his own cross.

The charge of the religious leaders against Jesus was blasphemy, but there was no Roman law against blasphemy. For this reason they convened a meeting very early in the morning in which they passed a resolution about what charges they would bring against Jesus that would be covered by Roman law. Mark, in his abbreviated form of writing does not tell us what the actual charges were, but we find them in Luke. He was to be charged with perverting the nation, and forbidding to give tribute to Caesar, and declaring that he was the Messiah—a king (Luke 23:2).

There were three people or groups that were involved in this trial: 1) The chief priests, who would represent the religious leadership, 2) Pontius Pilate, the Roman procurator, and 3) the crowd, some of whom lived in Jerusalem, but many also who had come into Jerusalem to celebrate the Passover.

1. The Priests

The priests were beginning to lose their control over the people. Jesus had been saying things that the people had known for a long time and they were glad at last to hear someone saying them publicly. The people had been delighted when Jesus had exposed the graft of the priests when he chased the money-changers out of the temple. Pilate knew that the priests were envious of Jesus (Mark 15:10).

The impromptu trial before Annas, the former high priest, and Caiaphas, the current high priest, had been illegal because it had been held in the middle of the night. It was unlawful to hold a trial that concerned somebody's life during the night. In addition to this, no trial for capital punishment could be initiated on the night of a major festival such as the Passover, and Jesus' trial before the chief priest had not ended until cock-crow, which would have been about three o'clock in the morning. He was kept in the house of Caiaphas from three until six in the morning and then taken to Pilate for the Roman trial. Roman officials started their day very early in the morning because they reserved the afternoon for recreation and leisure. That is why they had to get Jesus to Pilate very early. Everything the chief priests did throughout the night was totally illegal and, of course, they must have known it.

2. Pontius Pilate

Pilate actually lived in Caesarea, but he came to Jerusalem with a garrison of soldiers during any festive occasion in order to keep peace. Pilate asked Jesus directly, "Are you the King of the Jews?"

To this Jesus answered, "Thou sayest" (Matthew). "Thou sayest it" (Mark and Luke). "Sayest thou this thing of thyself, or did others tell it thee of me" (John). The gospel writers use slightly different words, but the answer is an unmistakable Yes.

However, when Jesus told Pilate the nature of his kingdom, Pilate was satisfied that Jesus was no threat to Rome: "My kingdom is not of this world: if my kingdom were of this world, then would my servants fight, that I should not be delivered to the Jews: but now is my kingdom not from hence" (John 18:36).

At this point Pilate made use of the Roman custom of releasing a political prisoner during the Passover. He told the people that they could choose between Barabbas and Jesus. Now Barabbas was an insurrectionist and murderer who perhaps even belonged to a group called the Sicarii—daggerbearers. This group specialized in murder and assassination. In our times they would have been terrorists. Without doubt Barabbas was a thug and would have been popular only amongst his own immediate group. Pilate was convinced that the people would not ask for a prisoner such as Barabbas to be released and a good teacher to be condemned. However, he was wrong. The people chose Barabbas and condemned Jesus.

Although technically Pilate had the power to veto the decision of the people, he was afraid to do so because it would have had serious political repercussions in Rome that would have ended his career. He did what any modern politician might have done. He allowed himself to be guided by the polls instead of doing the thing that he knew was right. He made a decision that was popular, but his name has gone down in history among the infamous. Nobody ever calls their son Pilate.

3. The Crowd

How the crowd could have changed so drastically in such a short time is hard to understand. Less than a week before this they had welcomed Jesus as he came into Jerusalem, crying out: "Hosanna; Blessed is he that cometh in the name of the Lord: Blessed be the kingdom of our father David, that cometh in the name of the Lord: Hosanna in the highest" (Mark 11:9-10).

Now they were crying out: "Crucify him! Crucify him!"

Some people think that it was the pilgrims from Galilee who had come in for the Passover that acclaimed him when he came into Jerusalem and it was citizens of Judaea who surrounded him when he was being tried by Pilate. This may be true, but it is more likely that these people were acting as any crowd. They were very easily influenced, and they wanted to follow a winner. As long as Jesus was healing the sick, raising the dead, cleansing lepers and holding crowds spellbound with his teaching, they were eager to follow him. However, they were not particularly interested in riding the bandwagon of one who had been betrayed, deserted by his three closest disciples and abandoned by all the rest of his disciples. Nor did they want to follow a man who was accused by the authorities.

This crowd was being very neatly manipulated by the public media of their day. The officials had convinced them that Barabbas was more valuable to them than Jesus. This is not suprising if we remember how easily our public media manipulates us today. Most of those who control the newspapers, radio and television in our society tend to be liberal in their outlook, so that the news we hear is often slanted to the left. The extreme leftwing of our media has some people convinced that the only people who help the poor are the communists. Many of the black people in South Africa are convinced that the only hope for freedom and help is the communist world.

Of course, this is a blatant lie, as can easily be seen by observing

145

conditions in the communistic countries themselves. There are no people in the world who have less liberty than the people in Russia, Albania, Yugoslavia, Romania and the other communistic countries of the world. There are very few countries outside of the Third World that have less consumer goods available to their people than the communistic countries. Real freedom in the communistic countries is only a dream. Their people are not even close to being free in reality.

At any rate, Jesus did not seem to be on the bandwagon of success any longer, and it was very easy for the Jewish leaders to convince the people that they ought to do away with him. One of the most remarkable things about these phony trials was the silence of Jesus—of course a fulfilment of prophecy: "He was oppressed, and he was afflicted, yet he opened not his mouth: he is brought as a lamb to the slaughter, and as a sheep before her shearers is dumb, so he openeth not his mouth" (Isa. 53:7).

There are at least five different kinds of silence. There is the silence of wonder and admiration. Sometimes the hush that comes over an audience after a particularly spectacular performance speaks much more loudly than any amount of applause. Sometimes the look in a wife's eyes speaks louder than words.

Then there is the silence of contempt. A person does not respond simply because the remark that was made is not worth answering.

The silence of fear can be a dreadful thing. This is the silence among the people in a country that is ruled by a malevolent dictator such as Adolph Hitler, Joseph Stalin, Idi Amin, or Muammar Quaddafi.

There is also the silence of a heart that is hurt. This is a sort of dumb sorrow in which someone has been injured to such an extent there are no words to express it.

Finally, there is the silence of tragedy. Nothing more can be said. There is no use talking any longer. It would be useless to go to the peace table again. This was the silence between Jesus and the chief priests. This was the silence between Jesus and Pontius Pilate. This is the silence between Jesus and the cold heart. This is what happened to Pharaoh when Moses was demanding that he let the people go. His heart had become so hard that nothing would ever change it again.

Jesus was silent before Pontius Pilate and the chief priests because there was nothing more to say. What a tragedy it is when a man reaches the point in his life when he is so relentlessly bitter against God that even God has nothing more to say to him. The day of "reasoning together" is over.

Dr. A. B. Simpson, the founder of the Christian and Missionary

Alliance, puts into poetry the decision with which Pilate was confronted:

Jesus is standing in Pilate's hall—
Friendless, forsaken, betrayed by all:
Harken! What meaneth the sudden call!
What will you do with Jesus?

Jesus is standing on trial still—
You can be false to him if you will,
You can be faithful through good or ill:
What will you do with Jesus?

What will you do with Jesus?
Neutral you cannot be;
Someday your heart will be asking,
"What will he do with me?"

Part Six

*Looking in the Wrong Places
for the Right Person—Chapter 16*

And when the sabbath was past, Mary Magdalene, and Mary the mother of James, and Salome, had bought sweet spices, that they might come and anoint him. And very early in the morning the first day of the week, they came unto the sepulchre at the rising of the sun. And they said among themselves, "Who shall roll us away the stone from the door of the sepulchre?" And when they looked, they saw that the stone was rolled away: for it was very great. And entering into the sepulchre, they saw a young man sitting on the right side, clothed in a long white garment; and they were affrighted. And he saith unto them, "Be not affrighted: Ye seek Jesus of Nazareth, which was crucified: he is risen; he is not here: behold the place where they laid him."

Mark 16:1-6

Chapter 16

Looking in the Wrong Places for the Right Person

These women had followed him throughout most of his preaching career. Now at the end they had followed him from Galilee to Judaea, from Nazareth to Jerusalem. They had seen him die. Their hopes were gone. Their dreams were destroyed. Their faith was shattered.

They had followed at a distance from the cross to the place of burial. They had watched as Joseph of Arimathaea and Nicodemus had prepared his body for the grave. Because the Sabbath was rapidly approaching, they had done it hastily but lavishly. They had used one hundred pounds of spices. Mary's alabaster bottle of perfume would have weighed only one pound, and yet Judas had calculated that it was worth as much as a man could earn in an entire year.

Finally, they had seen these two men groan and gasp as they had slowly rolled the heavy stone across the mouth of the tomb. The stone

151

had to be heavy so that thieves could not break in and steal the spices that had been used. Jews did not embalm bodies for burial. Instead, they used very strong spices to counteract the odor of decomposition. The tomb also had to be protected so that other people would not use it to bury other bodies. The stone might have been as much as six feet in width and perhaps thee or four feet in height.

These faithful women must have thought that they would never forget the dull thud of finality with which the stone dropped into place and sealed the tomb. Perhaps even then they wondered how they would be able to move the stone so that they could go in and add the touch of a woman's hands to the final preparation of the body of their Lord for that eternal sleep of eternal darkness. But the Sabbath was almost upon them. The sun had set and they had only a few minutes to get home and begin to wait through the longest Sabbath they had ever spent.

When the Sabbath came, there was almost total inactivity. It must have seemed endless to these women. They were anxious to go back to the tomb once more and perform a final act of love and kindness. There was Mary Magdalene, Mary the mother of James, Salome and Joanna. Patiently they waited all through that night and the long day that followed. Finally the Sabbath was over. The bazaars in the marketplace were open. They hurried out to buy the ointments with which they wanted to anoint their master's body one more time. Everything was now ready, but still they had to wait through the long hours of another night.

It was still dark when they set out, but by the time they got to the tomb, the sun was beginning to rise. One cannot help but wonder where the disciples were at this time. Of course, Judas was already in hell. Peter was in a hell of his own making, and the others had shut themselves in because they were afraid. Only these four women had the courage to venture forth. As they approached the tomb, they had an alarming thought. "Who will roll that huge stone away from the mouth of the grave so that we can go in?"

But they were worrying about something that God had already done. God solved the problem of the stone with an earthquake and an angel: "And, behold, there was a great earthquake: for the angel of the Lord descended from heaven, and came and rolled back the stone from the door, and sat upon it" (Matt. 28:2).

They were concerned about the enormous nature of the task and their own lack of ability to perform it. They had forgotten completely about the power of God. The children of Israel did exactly the same thing at the Red Sea. The sea was in front of them and the Egyptians were behind them. They complained to Moses: "Is not this the word that we did tell thee in Egypt, saying, Let us alone, that we may serve the Egyptians? For it had been better for us to serve the Egyptians, than that we should die in the wilderness" (Exod. 14:12).

Moses answered with words that have become to us one of the greatest texts in the Bible: "Fear ye not, stand still, and see the salvation of the Lord, which he will shew to you today: for the Egyptians whom ye have seen today, ye shall see them again no more forever. The Lord shall fight for you, and ye shall hold your peace" (Exod. 14:13-14).

Many times we feel exactly the same as these women must have felt. Who will roll away the stone? I feel that God is calling me to become a medical doctor or God wants me to be an executive businessman or God wants me to be a farmer, and so on? How will I ever do it? What can I do about this marriage? It seems to be falling apart. What is there left to live for? Our children seem to be going the wrong way. After all we have done to try and help them, to bring them up in the love and the admonition of the Lord, to turn their steps in the right direction . . . everything is going wrong. They have not responded. Somewhere we must have made a mistake, and so on.

We go to the funeral parlor to make the final arrangements for a loved one that has been taken from us. The usual mundane questions are asked. What kind of casket do you want? Of course you will want to do the best that you can for your mother. It would be nice if you were to get an outside container so that the moisture will be kept out and the level of the sod above will remain constant and not sink in. You will want to get a grave that is located in a pretty place where there is a good view. Remember that this is the last resting place of your mother.

Then we hear the monotonous tones of the minister's voice: "Earth to earth, dust to dust, ashes to ashes—in the joyful hope of the sure resurrection of all who die in Christ. 'O death where is thy sting? O grave where is thy victory . . . .' "

The world seems to have stopped as we stand there in a light drizzle on a foggy day looking for the last time at the box that contains our mother, and from a heart that has no answers, we say with the women at the tomb of Jesus, "Who shall roll us away the stone? Who shall roll us away the stone? Who shall roll us away the stone? . . ."

Then we hear a voice from another world: "Don't weep, my child. The stone has already been rolled away. Don't look at the stone. Look at the Savior."

Then, to their amazement, these women discovered that they were looking in the wrong place: "Be not affrighted: Ye seek Jesus of Nazareth, which was crucified: he is risen: he is not here: behold the place where they laid him" (Mark 16:6).

Suddenly they were desperately frightened and they ran away: "For they trembled and were amazed: Neither said they any thing to any man; for they were afraid" (Mark 16:8).

They had understood the man of Galilee. They were able to talk to the carpenter of Nazareth. He was human. He had exactly the same kind of accent as they did. They could handle the babe of Bethlehem. Some of them had been mothers themselves. They were able to cope with the martyr on the cross. They had expected this—it was the natural outcome of the animosity of the religious leaders. And they knew how to prepare the body for the grave. They had done this before.

But they were not able to deal with the miraculous. They had never been able to comprehend the God-man. When Jesus acted as a human they were able to take it in their stride, but when he acted as God they were frightened. Many months ago when he had calmed the storm he had said to them: "Why are ye so fearful? How is it that ye have no faith? And they feared exceedingly, and said one to another, What manner of man is this, that even the wind and the sea obey him" (Mark 4:40-41).

The people reacted in exactly the same way when Jesus cast the demons out of the Gadarene. They came out of the town to see what had happened and when they saw the man clothed and in his right mind they were afraid: "They [came] to Jesus, and see him that was possessed with the devil, and had the legion, sitting, and clothed, and in his right mind: and they were afraid" (Mark 5:15). They were not able to handle Jesus when he acted like God.

The woman who had had the incurable blood disease for twelve years had the same reaction. She was extremely frightened: "But the woman fearing and trembling, knowing what was done in her, came and fell down before him, and told him all the truth" (Mark 5:33). She could have coped with Jesus if he had been a great teacher or a prominent religious leader, but she was unable to deal with him when he acted as God.

The disciples cried out in fear when they saw him walking on the water: "But when they saw him walking upon the sea, they supposed it had been a spirit, and cried out: For they all saw him, and were troubled. And immediately he talked with them, and saith unto them, Be of good cheer: it is I; be not afraid" (Mark 6:49-50). If he had come to them in another boat, there would have been no problem whatsoever, but when they saw him walking on the water—doing something that only God could do—they were terrified.

Peter and James and John were gripped by this same fear when they

154

saw Jesus and Moses and Elijah on the Mount of Transfiguration: Not knowing what to say, Peter made some foolish remark about building three tabernacles, and the Bible says, "He wist not what to say; for they were sore afraid" (Mark 9:6). His great teaching they could understand, his profound insights delighted them, his comments about the Old Testament scriptures were music to their ears, but when he began acting as God, they could not handle it.

The Gospel of Mark leaves us on this note: "They went out quickly, and fled from the sepulchre; for they trembled and were amazed: neither said they anything to any man; for they were afraid" (Mark 16:8). Every time the God in the God-man took over, the people who were present shrank away from him in fear. I think this was because when they saw him as God, they saw themselves as sinners, and of course sinners cannot stand before a holy God. This is why many people have attempted to humanize Jesus. All through the history of the church there has been a constant effort to keep Jesus as a human—a very intelligent human, a very kind human, a very helpful human, a very discerning human, but a human. People are glad to concentrate upon Jesus as the baby or as the carpenter or as the teacher or even as the martyr, but don't let him be God!

This is where the Gospel of Mark ends. The last twelve verses that we have in our Bible are an addition by some other writer. It is an extremely old addition—dating back to the first century, but most scholars, including conservative evangelical scholars, agree that these verses were not written by the same man who wrote the rest of this Gospel.

There are some who think that Mark wrote a conclusion to the Gospel himself and that very early it was lost. I rather think that it was the nature of Mark to stop as abruptly as he did. He had finished what he wanted to say and I imagine he concluded that there was no point in adding anything else to it. However, what was added has done us no harm. It is quite in sympathy with the teaching of all the Gospels, and it makes a fitting conclusion. Each of the Gospel writers tells us some things that the others do not tell us. They each saw the events from their own standpoint.

However, the major events are absolutely uniform. Two of these that appear in every Gospel are the fact of the resurrection and the declaration of the Great Commission. Because Jesus rose from the grave, we have a message to give. Although they were added by someone other than Mark, the last two verses of the sixteenth chapter are pertinent: "So then after the Lord had spoken unto them, he was received up into heaven, and sat on the right hand of God. And they went forth, and preached everywhere, the Lord working with them, and confirming the word with signs following. Amen'' (Mark 16:19-20). Thus endeth the reading.